To Will and Houman

In memory of

Helen I. Harris

2007

Kiplinger's

Ask Kim for
Money
Smart
Solutions

WITHDRAWN
Kimberly Lankford

 **KAPLAN**) PUBLISHING

This publication is designed to provide accurate and authoritative information in regard to the subject matter covered. It is sold with the understanding that the publisher is not engaged in rendering legal, accounting, or other professional service. If legal advice or other expert assistance is required, the services of a competent professional should be sought.

Editorial Director: Jennifer Farthing
Acquisitions Editor: Victoria Smith
Production Editor: Michael Hankes
Production Artist: Virginia Byrne
Cover Designer: Gail Chandler

Published by Kaplan Publishing, a division of Kaplan, Inc.

Printed in the United States of America

07 08 09   10 9 8 7 6 5 4 3 2 1

For information about ordering Kaplan Publishing books at special quantity discounts, please call 1-800-KAP-ITEM or write to Kaplan Publishing, 888 Seventh Ave., 22nd Floor, New York, NY 10106.

Contents

Introduction

I love writing the Ask Kim column for *Kiplinger's Personal Finance Magazine* and Kiplinger.com because it gives me so much personal contact with our readers. It helps me learn exactly what they're interested in and gives me immediate feedback whenever I write an article. Because of this relationship, I've grown to know what the readers are looking for much better than most personal finance writers.

Readers seem to be craving this interaction. I receive about 15 to 20 questions every day—well over 5,000 per year—from people who take the time to write detailed letters about their financial situations. They seem to appreciate having someone who they've grown to know and trust answering their questions in a very approachable way. And they're very relieved to discover that other people are dealing with the same issues, and that they aren't alone.

That's why I'm so excited to finally write this book. I've been writing the column for nearly ten years and have answered almost every question readers have about personal finances—whether it's strategies to stretch their retirement savings, get help with astronomical college costs, find the best deals on their mortgage and insurance, climb out from under debt, or save money on their taxes. Many questions focus on financial hierarchy: with so many goals but limited money, what do you do first? How do you juggle college and retirement savings? What can you do to catch up if you haven't saved much yet? Some focus on the best steps to save money—whether it's on your insurance premiums, credit-card debt, or tuition bills. And others are more technical: how can I qualify for specific tax breaks, improve my credit score, or guarantee that I won't outlive my retirement income?

The good news is that there are straightforward answers to all of these questions—and many more. This book can be a wonderful resource that deals with all of your personal finance questions in every category—whether you're just getting started or know the basics but have follow-up questions about squeezing even more money out of your savings.

And it's timely. Several new tax laws, insurance developments, financial aid rules, and retirement-saving products were just introduced this year, which change some of the strategies. It's a perfect time to reassess your financial plans and make sure you're still on the right track.

This book is a great place to find answers to your questions about every major goal in your life and a road map for improving your financial situation. But it's not the final word. If you have follow-up questions about any of these topics, please e-mail me at *askkim@kiplinger.com.* I continue to write the column for *Kiplinger's Personal Finance Magazine* and Kiplinger.com and I am always looking for ways to help our readers. I'd love to hear from you.

Retirement Saving

I receive more questions from readers about retirement saving than any other financial goal. It's because the stakes are so high; the steps you take during your working years can make a huge difference in the way you live during the last few decades of your life. But it's also the area where you can get the most help—from the government, your employer, and your investments. If you know how to make the most of these tools, it becomes so much easier to reach your retirement-savings goals.

Hearing from so many readers also puts retirement planning into perspective. A lot of books focus on the theory of saving for retirement—how much money you *should* be setting aside. But it takes questions from real people to focus on the fact that it isn't always as easy as it sounds on paper. A lot of people can't afford to max out both their 401(k) and IRA. So if you only have so much money, what should you do first? And how can you get started with a small amount of savings? Or what if you've done very little through the years and are starting to worry about catching up?

The good news is that there are solid answers to all of these questions—great strategies to help you improve your retirement savings, no matter what you've done so far. And there are a lot of tools to help stretch your savings even further. Here's how to make the most of them.

How Much Do I Need and How Do I Get There?

How much do I need to save for retirement? Is $1 million enough?

Many people tend to throw up their hands when it comes to figuring out how much money they need to save for retirement. The numbers are so huge that it can seem like Monopoly money. When you're young, you don't need to worry too much about the specific figures; you just save as much as you can afford and keep adding to your retirement accounts whenever you can.

But there are actually some pretty simple calculations that can give you an idea of how much money you'd need to save for retirement, and how to figure out whether you're on the right track.

Start by taking your annual income and adjusting it until retirement for inflation—3 percent per year has been typical—to estimate your annual income just before you retire. Advisors tend to recommend that you have 75 percent to 85 percent of your preretirement income to live on in retirement—more if you still have a mortgage and plan to travel and lead an expensive lifestyle; less if you've paid off your home and your other regular expenses have dropped.

But you don't need to come up with all of that money on your own. Estimate how much money you'll get from sources other than your savings, such as Social Security and possibly a pension. Most people get 20 percent to 30 percent of their preretirement income from Social Security, which could leave you with as little as 50 percent of your preretirement income to come up with on your own. (You can get a more precise figure from your annual Social Security earnings statement or run your numbers through the benefits calculator at *www.ssa.gov*.) And if you're in line for a decent pension, you may need to come up with even less than 50 percent of your preretirement income yourself to fill in the gap.

Then, translate that annual income gap into a lump sum, which is surprisingly easy to do. Many advisors recommend that you withdraw only 4 percent of your retirement savings during the first year, and then adjust the future withdrawals for inflation. That's a conservative rule of thumb, but it's a good way to make sure you won't run out of money in retirement. Because that 4 percent represents 1/25 of your retirement money, you can come up with your needed nest egg by multiplying your income needs in the first year of retirement by 25.

If you need $40,000 per year to supplement Social Security and a pension in retirement, for example, your savings goal will be $1 million. You may need a bigger nest egg, however, if you don't have a pension and still have a mortgage.

I've heard that it's a good rule of thumb to save 10 percent of my income each year. Will that be enough to cover my retirement?

It depends on how old you are, how much you've already saved, and any guaranteed sources of income you have in retirement, such as a pension. The results can vary a lot.

A study by T. Rowe Price found that a 30-year-old would need to save 11 percent of his income per year to amass a lump sum that provides 70 percent of his current income in retirement (adjusted for inflation). The number rises to 21 percent if he waits until age 40 to start saving. But if that 40-year-old had already saved an amount equal to his annual salary, he'd only need to set aside another 14 percent per year.

To calculate your annual savings goal, figure out how big a nest egg you need (see the calculation on page 3), then work backwards. Starting early makes a big difference. If you're 25 years old and want to have $1 million for retirement, for example, you'll only need to invest about $3,600 per year to amass that much by age 65, if your investments return 8 percent per year. If you wait until age 30 to get started, you'll need to set aside about $5,400 per year to end up with the same $1 million at age 65. Starting at age 40 requires $12,700 per year to reach the magic million. And you'll need a whopping $34,000 per year to reach the same goal if you procrastinate until age 50.

Don't get too hung up on the specifics, especially if you're young. In general, younger workers will do well if they save 15 percent of their income each year, including their employer match. The key is to save early and often and boost your contributions whenever you can.

For help figuring out how much you need to save, first check out the "How Will Retirement Affect My Expenses?" calculator at Kiplinger.com, then run your numbers through the "Am I Saving Enough for Retirement?" calculator. For a more precise figure, plug your numbers into a calculator that uses Monte Carlo simulations, running through thousands of potential investment scenarios and assessing the likelihood that you'll reach your retirement goals, such as the one at FinancialEngines.com. (The program generally costs $149.95 per year, but some employers provide free access to the same calculators through their 401(k) advice programs.)

I barely have enough money to pay my bills. How can I afford to save for retirement?

It may be a lot easier than you'd expect. The IRS and most employers kick in some money to help you reach your goals, so you can set aside a substantial amount of money without taking much of a hit in your paycheck.

If you have a 401(k) with an employer match, you could get a lot of free money. If, for example, your employer matches 50 cents on the dollar for up to 6 percent of your salary and you earn $40,000, you'll get the maximum match if you contribute $2,400 in a 401(k). In that case, you'll get $1,200 from your employer, bringing your total contribution up to $3,600, just by contributing $2,400.

And that $2,400 doesn't lower your paycheck dollar for dollar, either, because you're investing the money before you pay taxes on it. If you're in the 25 percent bracket, investing $2,400 will only reduce your take-home pay by $1,800 for the year. So it actually costs you just $150 per month to end up with a $3,600 contribution every year. If you start doing that at age 30, you'll have about $670,000 by the time you're 65, if your investments return 8 percent per year.

If you also can afford to invest $200 per month in a Roth IRA, that brings your total savings rate up to 15 percent of your $40,000 salary. Continue to invest that much for 35 years and you could end up with more than $440,000 at age 65, which is totally tax free because it's in the Roth. Add the two together and you have more than $1.1 million for your retirement. To qualify for a Roth IRA, you must earn less than $166,000 in 2007 if married filing jointly; or $114,000 if single.

That's a big chunk of your savings goal, but may not be enough to cover all of your retirement needs—especially if you start saving after age 30. Keep adding more money to your retirement savings whenever you get a raise or bonus at work or a big gift. That way, you'll invest the money before you get used to having it. In 2007, you can contribute up to $15,500 in a 401(k) ($20,500 if you're 50 or older) and $4,000 to an IRA ($5,000 if 50 or older).

If you can start maxing out your 401(k) and IRA at age 40 and continue at that pace for the next 25 years, you could end up with more than $1.5 million in retirement savings by age 65, if your investments return 8 percent per year. That's in addition to any retirement savings you set aside before then.

Don't have anywhere near that much money? Even a little bit can add up, especially when you're young. Investing just $100 per month into a Roth IRA can add up to $1,200 by the end of the year. And if you're 30 now, keep up that savings pace for the next 35 years, and your investments earn 8 percent annually, then you'll have more than $220,000 in tax-free money by the time you're 65—just by investing $100 per month.

I'm 30 years old and earn about $30,000 per year. Most of my paychecks go toward my apartment, student loans, and car payments. I'd like to start saving for retirement, but don't have a lot of money to invest. Which should I do first—invest in my 401(k) at work or open up a Roth IRA?

f your employer matches your 401(k) contributions, then that should be your first saving priority; it's free money that you won't get anywhere else. And because your 401(k) contributions lower your taxable income, they won't reduce your take-home pay by nearly as much as you'd expect.

Then, invest up to $4,000 pear year ($333 per month) into a Roth IRA. You can't deduct your Roth contributions, but you can make tax-free withdrawals in retirement. Because you're in a low tax bracket now—and likely to be in a higher bracket later—you'll benefit more from the Roth IRA's tax-free growth than you would from the current tax deduction you'd get with your 401(k) contribution. The Roth also provides other valuable benefits: You can withdraw your contributions at any time without paying taxes or a penalty, you can withdraw earnings without penalty to pay for college expenses, and after your account has been open for at least five years, you can withdraw $10,000 in earnings tax and penalty free to buy a first home. Your heirs can inherit a Roth IRA tax free and, unlike traditional IRAs, you don't have to take required distributions at age 70½.

If you max out your Roth IRA, invest any remaining money in your 401(k), which gives you a current tax break and grows tax-deferred until retirement. The contribution limit is $15,500 in 2007 if you're 50 or younger. You may be far from maxing out your account now, but keep adding extra money whenever income increases or your expenses decrease. After you pay off your student loans and car, for example, use the extra cash to boost your retirement contributions.

My spouse and I max out our 401(k) accounts. We're not eligible to use Roth IRAs because of income restrictions. Does it make sense to invest in regular IRAs for additional retirement-oriented savings or is there another place to better park that type of money?

You ask a very timely question. Until very recently, we weren't too keen on nondeductible IRAs. If you earned too much money to qualify for a Roth ($114,000 for singles; $166,000 for married couples filing jointly in 2007) and couldn't deduct your contributions, we generally recommended that people invest in taxable accounts rather than traditional IRAs. That way, they'd have fewer restrictions on accessing the money and they'd be taxed at a lower rate when they withdrew it in retirement. Traditional IRA withdrawals are taxed at your income-tax rate, which can be as high as 35 percent, while stocks or funds held in a taxable account (a regular brokerage or fund account) are taxed at your long-term capital gains rate, which is 15 percent or lower.

That's still a compelling reason to invest in taxable accounts, especially if you minimize your trades or stick with funds that don't create many taxable distributions each year.

But nondeductible IRAs now do look a bit more interesting, because Congress passed a tax law that will eventually give you a back door to use a traditional IRA to get into a Roth if you wouldn't otherwise qualify. The new law, which goes into effect in 2010, keeps the Roth income limits the same (you still won't be able to contribute if you're single earning more than $114,000 or $166,000 if you're married filing jointly in 2007). But it eliminates the $100,000 income limit for converting a traditional IRA to a Roth.

That means you can start contributing to a traditional IRA now, and then in 2010 you'll be able to convert that traditional IRA into a Roth. At that point, you'll have to pay income taxes on your earnings at your top rate, but any earnings after that will come out tax free in retirement after age 59½, as long as the account has been opened for at least five years. If you convert in 2010, you'll be able to spread the tax bill over 2011 and 2012.

There also are other benefits to switching to a Roth. You'll avoid having to take required mandatory distributions at age 70½, which are required with a traditional IRA, and your heirs can inherit a Roth tax free.

Should I invest in a Roth 401(k) if my employer offers one at work?

A Roth 401(k) offers all the tax-free advantages of a Roth IRA but with the higher contribution limits of a 401(k)—$15,500 for most workers and $20,500 for those 50 and older in 2007. And there are no income limits, unlike a Roth IRA, which is only available to married couples filing jointly who earn less than $166,000, or single filers earning less than $114,000. So if you are shut out of funding a Roth IRA because you make too much money, this could be your opportunity to build up a stash of tax-free income for retirement.

The downside is that you don't get a tax deduction for contributing to a Roth 401(k), so switching could mean a big tax hit. In the 28 percent bracket, for example, you'd owe $5,740 in taxes on a $20,500 contribution. And your take-home pay would be reduced compared with the same contribution to a traditional 401(k) plan.

There's no predicting what tax rates will be when you stop working, so the prospect of tax-free income in retirement is a good way to diversify your savings. One strategy is to split your contributions between the two types of 401(k) plans (as long as your combined contribution doesn't exceed the annual maximum). That way, you can preserve some of your tax deductions and accumulate tax-free income for the future.

I'm 50 and still haven't saved much for retirement. What can I do to catch up?

The younger you are when you start saving, the less money you'll have to set aside to reach the same goal. That's great in theory. But what if you'd been spending all of your money on college and a mortgage and hadn't started saving for retirement until later? There's still some hope for you.

First, make the most of catch-up contributions. The IRS has special rules to help people in exactly your situation. Instead of an annual 401(k) limit of $15,500, workers age 50 and older can contribute $20,500 to their 401(k)s in 2007. You'll also be able to contribute an extra $1,000 to your IRA—giving you a total contribution limit of $5,000 for 2007. Start maxing out these retirement plans now and you can still amass a decent-sized nest egg by the time you retire. Saving $25,500 each year will give you nearly $750,000 in your 401(k) and IRA by the time you're 65, if your investments return 8 percent per year.

That probably won't cover your entire retirement, but it's a step in the right direction. Invest any additional money in a taxable account that you use to buy and hold stocks or funds for the long term, minimizing the annual tax bill, and save extra money whenever your expenses shrink; for example, if you finally stop paying your kids' college costs or you cut back on life insurance.

And there's an easy way to amass even more money: don't retire at age 65. Even working just part-time after that will do wonders for your retirement savings. You won't start tapping your retirement savings for a few more years, you may even be able to keep saving more money, and your nest egg will need to last for fewer years. Plus, delaying your Social Security benefits beyond age 62 will increase your payouts for the rest of your life. According to a study by T. Rowe Price, if you earn $100,000 at age 65, have $500,000 in savings and save 10 percent of your salary each year, working for just two extra years can increase your retirement income by 26 percent. Working for four extra years can increase your retirement income by 59 percent.

How IRAs and 401(k)s Work

I'm currently saving in my Roth IRA and company 401(k) and have maxed them out. I also have a part-time consulting job for a nonprofit. It has started a 403(b) to which I am required to make mandatory contributions of 2.5 percent; the nonprofit will contribute 5 percent. How will that impact my other retirement savings vehicles? Can I contribute to all three accounts?

Y ou can contribute to all three accounts, but there are limits on the amounts. In 2007, you can contribute up to $15,500 to your 401(k) and 403(b) combined (or $20,500 if you are 50 or older), so you'll need to coordinate your contribution amounts. Consider the matching rules for each plan before deciding where to cut back.

And your Roth IRA is subject to separate limits. As long as you earn less than $156,000 in 2007 if married filing jointly ($99,000 if single), you can contribute up to $4,000 to a Roth IRA, or $5,000 if 50 or older. You can contribute part of the limit until your income reaches $166,000 (or $114,000 for singles).

I opened my Roth IRA at Vanguard in 1998 when I was single. I married in 2000 and left my job in October 2005 to be a stay-at-home mom for a few years. I am not collecting income. Do I have to shift my Roth IRA to a spousal IRA?

Good news: not only are you smart to contribute to a spousal IRA, but you also don't need to open a new account to do it. As long as the adjusted gross income on your joint return is less than $166,000 per year, you can continue to contribute to your Vanguard Roth IRA, whether you qualify based on your own income or as a spouse.

You generally need earned income to contribute to a Roth IRA, but if your husband is employed, he can contribute up to $4,000 this year to a spousal Roth IRA on your behalf (or a bit less if your adjusted gross income is from $156,000 to $166,000). Because you already have a Roth IRA with Vanguard, you don't need to open a new account.

I am retired and have no earned income, but my wife is still working and has earned income. Does her earned income qualify me to start a Roth IRA? We file jointly and the earned income is less than $150,000.

Most people think of spousal IRAs for stay-at-home parents. But you've got the right idea: even though you generally need earned income to contribute to an IRA, your wife can make spousal IRA contributions for you as long as she earns more than she contributes to both accounts—$5,000 for each account if you're 50 or older in 2007.

To qualify for the Roth IRA, the adjusted gross income on your joint tax return must be less than $166,000 in 2007 (the contribution amount starts to phase out at $156,000). You can contribute to a Roth IRA at any age and won't have to make withdrawals even after you turn 70½.

I was thinking about starting a Roth IRA for my young son. However, I was wondering if there are any restrictions, such as does he have to earn the money?

That's a great idea. Investing in a Roth IRA for your child is an excellent way to give him a huge head start on saving for the future.

But there's one big catch: the child needs to have earned income—even if it's just from delivering newspapers, babysitting, or mowing lawns (but not just from his regular allowance). If your son's too young to earn money—and hasn't started a career as a baby model— then you'll need to find some other ways to save for now.

As soon as your son does earn money, opening a Roth IRA for him can be a very powerful way to save. He'll be able to invest the amount of his earned income, up to $4,000 in 2007, just like anyone else under age 50. (Those are the 2007 limits; the maximum increases every few years.) He doesn't need to invest the exact same money that he's earned himself; most 12-year-olds would have a tough time understanding why everything they earned has to be set aside for the future. As long as he has a job, you can give him some money to invest in the account, as long as it doesn't exceed the maximum limits.

Even investing just a little money in the account when he's young can make a big difference in the future. If you invest $2,000 when he's 12 in a Roth IRA and the investments earn 8 percent per year, that one contribution will grow to more than $100,000 by the time he's 67 years old. Continue to invest just that much every year, and his account will grow to about $2 million by retirement. Invest the maximum, now $4,000 and increasing, and he'll be a multimillionaire—tax free. What a great path on which to start your kid.

When your son starts to earn money, have him keep records that list the date of each job, the person who paid him, and how much he earned, and then keep the records in your tax files, just in case the IRS ever has questions.

Some IRA administrators give parents a tough time when they try to open an IRA for their kids because minors can't legally enter into binding contracts. But most fund companies and brokerage firms just require an adult to cosign the paperwork. Charles Schwab, Merrill Lynch, T.D. Waterhouse, Vanguard, T. Rowe Price, Dodge & Cox, and Oakmark, for example, all allow kids to open Roth IRAs.

I know that the 401(k) limit for people younger than age 50 this year is $15,500. I want to follow this limit, but my company sets a contribution limit based on a percentage of my income, which makes my limit lower than $15,500. Can they do this?

The company can allow it, but it may actually be a mistake. The key is to ask your employer about the reason for the percentage limit.

The most common explanation is because of "non-discrimination rules." By law, companies cannot have a situation where highly compensated employees (currently those earning more than $100,000) contribute a lot more to their 401(k)s than the rest of the employees. As a result, some employers set a limit on the percentage of income that can be contributed to prevent this situation.

If this is the case, see if your employer can do anything to encourage more lower-income employees to contribute to the plan. A 2006 tax law made it easier for companies to enroll employees automatically in their 401(k)s (with an opt-out option), which can satisfy the nondiscrimination rules without limiting employees' contributions, says Bob D. Scharin, editor of RIA's *Practical Tax Strategies*.

Another possible explanation: some of the percentage limits are just outdated rules. Before 2001, the employee's 401(k) contribution plus the employer match could not be more than 25 percent of a worker's income, so some employers capped their employee contributions at 15 percent to make sure they fell within those limits, says Rick Meigs, president of 401khelpcenter.com.

But in 2001, that limit was increased from 25 percent to 100 percent. "For all purposes, the plan limit was no longer necessary, but many plans never removed them," says Meigs.

Employers aren't required to make a change, but it's worthwhile to ask. If that's the only reason for the limits, see if the plan documents could be updated to eliminate the cutoff.

I got a new job. What should I do with my 401(k)?

The worst thing you can do is cash out your balance, which is what nearly half of all workers do when they switch jobs. If you are 30 years old and have a 401(k) balance of $20,000 earning a conservative

6 percent annually, your account would be worth more than $129,999 when you turn 62—assuming you don't make any additional contributions. If you spent that money today instead, you'd give up more than $100,000 in future earnings.

You have three better choices. As long as your balance is at least $5,000, you can keep the account with your old employer. Or, no matter how much you have in your account, you can roll it over to an IRA, or transfer it to your new employer's plan. An IRA would let you control the money yourself and give you the widest range of investment options. Transferring the money to your new company's plan would give you the convenience of having your retirement assets in one place. Not sure what to do? Keep the money with your old employer temporarily, especially if you like your current investments.

If you decide to move your money to a new account, have the check made out to the new trustee rather than to yourself. Otherwise, your employer is required to withhold 20 percent for taxes.

I am 26 years old and recently quit my job to further my education. I have a little over $7,000 in a 401(k) from the job. Additionally, I have about $3,000 in a 5-year-old Roth IRA. I'm aware of the IRA rollover option, but I was wondering if it would be possible to pay the tax on the 401(k) and combine it with my Roth IRA?

It's an excellent idea to roll over your 401(k) to a Roth IRA. Even though you'll have to pay income taxes on the converted amount, you'll come out ahead in the long run because you'll have decades of earnings that will all come out tax free in retirement.

It would be best, however, if you waited until you are in school next year to make the change, when your income—and tax bracket—will be lower and you can minimize the tax you have to pay on the conversion. In the 25 percent tax bracket, converting $8,000 to a Roth IRA would cost you $2,000 in federal taxes. But if you are in the 15 percent bracket next year, it will only cost $1,200 and if you're in the 10 percent bracket, just $800.

Previously, you had to roll over your 401(k) to a traditional IRA and then convert the traditional IRA to a Roth and pay the tax on the conversion. A new tax law will allow a direct rollover to a Roth IRA starting in 2008, but you still will have to pay taxes.

I recently withdrew funds from a Roth IRA and received a check in the mail. I deposited the money into my checking account, and then into another Roth IRA. Will I be penalized for making this withdrawal?

You shouldn't be penalized as long as you reinvested the money in another Roth IRA within 60 days. But you could have streamlined the process by having the money transferred directly from one IRA administrator to another.

The first Roth IRA custodian does not know that you rolled over the funds into a second IRA. So it will report the withdrawal to the IRS, and come January you'll receive a Form 1099-R showing the amount. You'll need to report the amount on your tax return, but don't treat it as a taxable distribution.

Next time, tell your new IRA administrator that you'd like to make a direct transfer. They're generally very happy to help with the paperwork because they'll be getting your money.

I was wondering if there is any downside to considering contributions toward a Roth as an emergency fund stash? My understanding is that withdrawals of contributions are penalty free.

You're right about the tax laws; you can withdraw your Roth contributions without a penalty or tax bill at any time, so your Roth could act as a source of emergency money in a pinch. You can also withdraw your earnings penalty free for college expenses and, after your account has been open for five years, you can withdraw up to $10,000 tax and penalty free to purchase a first home.

But there is a big downside. Once you remove the money from the Roth for longer than 60 days, you can't ever put it back in, so you'd lose years of tax-free growth by withdrawing the money before retirement.

You can only contribute up to $4,000 per year to a Roth IRA ($5,000 if you're 50 or older), and only if you earn less than $156,000 in 2007; $99,000 if single. Married couples can contribute part of the limit until their income reaches $166,000 (or $114,000 for singles).

If you withdraw this year's $4,000 contribution now to pay for emergency expenses, for example, you won't owe taxes or a penalty. But if you'd kept that money in the account for 25 years instead, then the $4,000 could have grown to be more than $27,000 if your investments returned 8 percent per year—giving you $23,000 of tax-free money you wouldn't have if you withdrew the $4,000 contribution.

It's better to keep three to six months of living expenses in a separate emergency fund, which can earn some interest and be easily accessible in an emergency. For the highest-earning money-market accounts, see the Yields & Rates page at Kiplinger.com.

If the company I work for goes bankrupt, would my 401(k) assets be affected? Do the same rules that apply to pensions apply to 401(k)s?

Money in a 401(k) can actually be considered safer in the event of an employer bankruptcy than money in a company pension plan. The money in a 401(k) must be held in a trust the employer can't touch, even if it's having financial trouble.

In some cases, however, employers have raided 401(k) money after it was deducted from employee paychecks but before it was deposited into the trust. "In instances where companies fail to put the assets in trust in a timely manner, we take action to enforce the law," says Assistant Secretary of Labor Ann Combs.

If you suspect a problem with your employer, contact the Labor Department's Employee Benefits Security Administration at 866-444-3272. The agency has recovered more than $700 million for participants in 401(k)s and similar savings plans.

The best way to protect yourself from an employer bankruptcy is to diversify your 401(k) investments rather than load up on your company's stock in your account.

Several months ago, our office manager left to work for another firm. Prior to leaving, she was having trouble keeping up with our 401(k) payments. I inquired several times about missing funds in my 401(k) and as a result I was able to get payments submitted. But after she left, things got worse. I've raised the issue with the CEO several times and I've been told the problem is being worked on. Is there anything I can do to ensure timelier 401(k) payments by my company?

It was a good idea to start by complaining to the CEO, but it sounds like you need more leverage. Next time, tell him you know the law: employers must get the money into your account within 15 business days after the end of the month of the contribution.

If your employer isn't doing this, contact the Department of Labor's Employee Benefits Security Administration. It's best to call 866-444-3272 and explain your situation to a benefits advisor.

The agency will look into your complaint and might be able to straighten things out, with or without taking the case to court. In the end, you and other workers could win payments for lost earnings. The agency has recovered more than $500 million in delinquent employee contributions.

How to Invest Retirement Money

I used to hear that the percentage of stocks in your portfolio should equal 100 minus your age. Is that still the case?

That's a good start to make sure you aren't too conservative, but you should generally invest even more aggressively. A 55-year-old, for example, should have a lot more than 45 percent of his retirement portfolio invested in stocks, because he could still live for 40 years or more. Stocks perform better than other investments over the long run, and you still have time to weather the market's ups and down.

A better version of the rule of thumb starts with 110 minus your age times 1.25. In that case, a 55-year-old would keep about 69 percent of his portfolio in stocks. If you have a pension that provides guaranteed income,

you can include that in the fixed portion of your portfolio, allowing the rest of your investments to be more
aggressive. But even that rule can be too conservative.

In fact, *Kiplinger's* recommended mutual fund portfolio keeps 100 percent of the money invested in stock
funds if you're ten years or more away from retirement.
When you're five to ten years away from retirement,
you have less time to bounce back from a market down-
turn, so the *Kiplinger's* portfolio shifts 30 percent of the
money into a bond fund, but still keeps 70 percent in
stock funds. And even after retirement, it still keeps 50
percent in stock funds, although less aggressive versions
than the ones recommended for young savers. (For
details about the specific funds, see the Investing section of Kiplinger.com.)

And that's just for retirement investing. The problem
with the age-based rule of thumb is that it assumes all of
your money is in your retirement savings. But instead,
you're probably juggling several goals, such as college savings, home buying, and saving for other major expenses.
Invest that money separately based on the time frame of
each of your goals, with college money invested aggressively when your child is ten or more years away from
school, and then gradually becoming more conservative
as he makes his way through high school.

**My wife and I are trying to determine the best
choice for her Roth IRA. We are 35 years old and
willing to accept some risk over the long term, and
we want to diversify our retirement savings. How
should we invest the money?**

You're definitely on the right track. The key words
are risk and diversify. Even though 100 percent
of the Kiplinger's long-term savings portfolio is
invested in stock funds, the money is spread out over

several types of stock funds, which helps minimize the risk. The model portfolio keeps about 50 percent of the money in funds that invest in large companies, split between stock funds that focus on fast-growing companies and half in bargain-priced ones (value funds). About 25 percent is in small-company stock funds, and 25 percent in foreign funds. This diversification should smooth out some of the bumpiness through the years, because it's unlikely that all types of companies will have a tough year at the same time.

And you should continue to be diversified, even as you gradually shift to more-conservative investments through time. When you're five years from your goal, the *Kiplinger's* model portfolio shifts money from a risky emerging growth fund and into a less-aggressive, dividend-oriented stock fund, and moves 30 percent of the money into a bond fund that invests in all kinds of bonds.

If your 401(k) doesn't offer exactly the same funds in the *Kiplinger's* portfolios, don't worry. Look at which category each fund is in—such as large-company growth, small-company value—and diversify with the funds you have available. If your 401(k) has some poor investment choices in the categories you need, you can diversify among all of your retirement investments, investing your IRA money in some of the categories and your 401(k) money in others. Just be sure to look across all of your retirement investments every year or so and rebalance your portfolio so you don't end up with too much money in one category of fund.

My best friend's little sister just graduated from college. She is just starting out in the working world and trying to get on her feet. It will be a while before she has a chunk of "extra" money with which to start investing. What I would like to do is help her set up an IRA. Once an account is set up, it is a lot easier to get in the habit of thinking of it and putting money in it. I should know. I procrastinated for several years and with IRAs the power of time is really the advantage. Do you have any suggestions on how to set up an IRA with minimal initial deposit?

What a great idea! If only everyone had a helpful friend to get them started. One good choice with a low minimum is T. Rowe Price Spectrum Growth (PRSGX), which lets you invest as little as $50 per month if you make automatic transfers from your bank account.

Spectrum Growth is a fund of funds investing in ten other T. Rowe Price stock funds, with money in a variety of large and small companies and foreign firms. It's an easy way to have a diversified long-term portfolio without worrying about meeting the minimum investment requirements of several funds.

The fund charges no extra fees (some funds of funds do), but just passes on the expenses of the funds in which it invests, which never total more than 1 percent per year.

Because she's just getting started, she'll probably qualify to invest in a Roth IRA, which will let her access the contributions at any time and withdraw the earnings totally tax free after age 59½ (you must earn less than $114,000 in 2007 to qualify if single; $166,000 if married).

The results can be huge by the time she retires. If she's 25 now and she invests $3,000 per year in an IRA every year until she's 65, she'll have amassed a nest egg of about $840,000, if the returns average 8 percent per year. Very impressive, considering that's from only investing $250 per month!

Also encourage her to invest first in a 401(k) at least up to the employer match, if available at her job, which provides free money that's tough to beat.

What's the best way to invest my IRA money without having to worry about monitoring my investments?

The easiest way to invest your retirement money is through a life-cycle fund. These funds invest in a portfolio of funds based on your time frame, and adjust the investments as your goal gets closer. They start out with more money invested in stock funds—when you have decades before you plan to touch the money—and then gradually become more conservative and move more money into bond funds and cash when you're about to start making withdrawals.

The life-cycle fund shifts the investments automatically; you don't need to make any changes yourself. Think about how long you'd like to keep the money invested, and then find a life-cycle fund that ripens on that date. If you're investing the money for retirement and you're currently in your mid-30s, consider one with a target date of 2035, or later if you plan on working longer.

When picking a life-cycle fund, be very careful about fees. Because they're funds of funds, they can have two layers of fees—those for the funds and an additional expense on top. It's best to focus on ones charging 2 percent or less, and staying under 1 percent is even better. And check out the performance of the underlying funds. Take a look at American Century, Fidelity, T. Rowe Price, and Vanguard. Each fund firm has slight variations on its stock versus bond allocation. T. Rowe Price's fund invests more heavily in stock funds in the early years than the others and tends to come closest to the portion that *Kiplinger's* recommends in its retirement-savings portfolios.

Because the fund is already diversified, you don't need to invest your IRA money in any other funds.

My son is in the Army in Iraq. He has no investments to speak of and is single. He wants to put much of his income into some form of investment, most likely a mutual fund due to the lack of communications. Do you have any advice for him for selecting a fund? His time to read is very limited.

Because your son is in the Army, he has an even better option for his retirement savings. Members of the military are eligible for the Thrift Savings Plan (TSP), which is like a 401(k) for federal employees. Money invested into that plan lowers your taxable income and grows tax deferred until you withdraw the money in retirement.

While he's deployed, his income is probably tax free anyway, but he'll still get benefits when he withdraws the money. When it's time to make a withdrawal, a proportionate share of taxable and tax-exempt money will be taken from his account. Tax-exempt money he puts in comes out tax free, and earnings on his tax-exempt contributions continue to grow tax deferred. Plus any bonuses and combat pay he receives aren't subject to the regular contribution caps. For more information about the tax rules for combat pay invested in a TSP, see the government's Thrift Savings Plan Web site (*www.tsp.gov*).

In fact, the government TSP just started offering life-cycle funds, which can be a great option for your son. He can pick the fund that matches his retirement date, then leave it in there for years.

Self-Employed Retirement Plans

What's the best retirement plan if I'm self-employed?

Self-employed people have several special retirement plans from which to choose, including a simplified employee pension (SEP), a Keogh, a SIMPLE, or an individual 401(k). All of the plans let you deduct your contributions from your income and the money grows tax deferred in retirement.

The SEP is usually the easiest to set up; most fund companies and brokerage firms that offer IRAs generally offer SEPs, and you usually have the same range of investment choices. But your contributions are limited to 20 percent of your income (business income minus half of your self-employment tax), up to $45,000.

An individual 401(k), also called a solo 401(k), gives you much higher contribution limits. You can contribute up to $15,500 in 2007 as an employee. Then, your business can kick in another 20 percent of your self-employment income (defined as total business income minus half of your self-employment tax), or 25 percent of your compensation if your business is incorporated. Because you're both the employer and the employee of your own business, that gives you a combined maximum contribution of $45,000 in 2007 (if you're 50 or older, you can contribute up to $50,000). You can only qualify for an individual 401(k) if you're the business's only employee (and your spouse, if employed by your business, too). These plans aren't available at all fund companies and brokerage firms, and some of the administrators charge high fees and have limited investment choices. However, several big companies, such as Fidelity, offer low-cost individual 401(k)s. For a list of providers, go to *www.401khelpcenter.com.*

Finding a Lost Pension

I was a Wal-Mart employee from 1988 to 1995 in a store that has since closed, and I'm trying to find out exactly what happened to my profit-sharing fund. I never received payment and I am wondering if it is too late to do anything about this. I have attempted to contact Wal-Mart, but the recording at the participant service center says that my Social Security number is not valid. Do you have any advice?

You're lucky that it's Wal-Mart. Because the company still exists, it's much easier to track down information about an old retirement plan than it can be from smaller employers or companies that have merged or disappeared.

Instead of calling the participant service center, which is more helpful for current employees, it's best to e-mail the company's benefits department at *benefitsonline @wal-mart.com* with your name, Social Security number, dates of employment, and store where you worked (give them the store number, and let them know that it's now closed). Then they'll be able to investigate your case and give you the status of your profit-sharing money.

Ask for the summary plan description that was in effect when you left the job, and the current one if different, plus the most recent individual benefit statement, says John Hotz, deputy director of the Pension Rights Center. Employers must provide that information within 30 days of your request, and Hotz recommends sending a certified letter to document the date. If you don't receive the information within that time frame, you can complain to the Department of Labor's Employee Benefits Security Administration (call 866-444-3272 to be connected to your regional office; the EBSA Web site, *www.dol.gov/ebsa*, also has helpful information).

The situation gets more complicated for companies that no longer exist. If you are faced with this situation, you'll need to do some detective work. You may be able to find the plan administrator by looking up the company at FreeERISA.com's database of Form 5500 filings, which companies must submit to the government with information about their retirement plans. The basic search is free, but you'll have to register at the site. If you can't reach the plan administrator, contact the service provider or trustee, also listed on the forms, who could help lead you in the right direction. If you can't find the plan's filings, FreeERISA.com generally charges $50 to search through older plan documents, or you can request the information from the EBSA's public disclosure room (call 866-444-3272 for information).

You may also be able to get help from the Pension Information and Counseling Project, which provides pension help in 25 states. For more information, see the Pension Rights Center's Web site (*www.pensionrights.org*).

College Planning

Anyone with kids knows a lot about juggling—whether it's your schedule or your savings goals. Not only do you have to spend money on child care and a lot of stuff as your kid grows up, but you also have that nagging worry in the back of your head wondering how you're going to pay the astronomical cost of college. Or, more often, how can you pay for college without jeopardizing your own retirement plans?

There actually are solid answers to these questions that will show you just how much money you'll give up in retirement if you divert all of your savings toward college, how big of a difference you can make if you start saving when your kid is young, and ways to make up for lost time if your child is about to graduate and you still have very little in his college fund.

Just like with retirement savings, the government provides help through tax-free college funds, tax-deductible student loans, and several tax credits for college tuition. If you know the rules, you can get a lot of free money from Uncle Sam to pay for your kid's education. And you have many more options than retirement savers do—scholarships, grants, loans, work-study, and other sources of cash to pay the bill.

But many of these rules changed significantly in the past year and it's an important time to reassess your college-savings plan, even if you thought you were off to a good start. New tax laws and financial aid formulas have totally changed the best strategies. Here's how to master the new world of college saving.

How Much Do You Need to Save?

I just saw this year's figures for the cost of college. How much will it cost by the time my 2-year-old son reaches college age? How much should I be saving now?

The numbers are unbelievably huge when you look at the total cost of college. According to the College Board, average tuition at a public college was $5,836 for the 2006–2007 school year, or $12,796 when you add in room and board. And the average tuition was $22,218 at a private college, or $30,367 with room and board.

With those numbers, the cost of four years would total more than $50,000 at a public college and $120,000 at a private school. And that's in today's dollars. If college costs continue to rise by about 5 percent per year, the total bill at a public college could top $125,000 by the time a newborn goes to school; or $300,000 at a private college. And that's just for one kid!

The good news is that you don't really have to pay that much money. If you start saving early and make the most of the help from the government, you can amass a big chunk of money without too much pain.

How much should you set aside? Saving $2,500 per year (less than $210 per month) will give you more than

$100,000 in 18 years, if your investments average 8 percent per year—almost enough to pay for four years at a public college. Setting aside $5,000 per year could grow to more than $200,000 in 18 years. If you also invested a lump sum of $20,000 when the child was born (which becomes a little easier to do if you ask relatives to contribute to the college fund rather than give big gifts), you'd have nearly enough money to pay full freight for four years at a private college.

But hardly anybody pays the full cost, so even saving a portion of that money can make a big difference. Between scholarships, grants, loans, tax credits, work-study, other money your child earns, and current cash flow (especially if you're used to paying for private high school), you don't need to save that much money for college. In fact, families received more than $135 billion in financial aid in the 2005–2006 school year. If you know the right strategies, your child can go to college at just a fraction of the cost.

I have two children, ages 2 and 5, and fear the incredibly high college costs I'll probably have to pay. I know that I should start saving for those costs now, but I only have so much money available every month, and I also know how important it is to save for my own retirement. Should I cut back on my retirement savings over the next few years in order to build up their college savings? I can't seem to be able to afford to do both.

That is probably the number one question I receive from readers. Everyone has multiple goals, with college and retirement being the biggies. It's tempting to help your kids, but don't put saving for your kids' college ahead of saving for your own retirement.

Your kids have plenty of alternatives—scholarships, financial aid, low-interest loans, a cheaper college, working while in school, or taking a year off while they save money. But you don't have any of these options for your own future. If you run out of money in retirement, there are no scholarships to help you fill in the gaps.

A study by T. Rowe Price illustrated how devastating bungling these priorities can be to your future financial security. If a couple earning $100,000 doesn't save anything for college but invests 6 percent of their income every year into their 401(k) and receives a 50 percent match from their employer, they'll have $2.5 million in retirement after 36 years (before taxes), if their investments return 8 percent per year. But they won't have any college savings.

On the opposite side of the spectrum, if they divert half of their potential retirement savings to college savings for 18 years, they'd have $253,000 in the college fund, but only have $759,000 saved for retirement.

A much better compromise is to save for both goals simultaneously. If you split your savings between college and retirement for the first 18 years, then save solely for retirement for the next 18 years, you'll end up with $126,000 in college savings—which can still cover a big chunk of your costs—but still have $1.65 million saved for retirement.

In a pinch, you could tap your retirement funds to help with college by borrowing against your 401(k) or by withdrawing your contributions to your Roth IRA (you can withdraw Roth IRA contributions tax- and penalty-free). You can even get penalty-free access to earnings on your Roth if you use the money for college expenses, though you'll still pay taxes on the earnings.

But before you dip into your retirement funds, investigate scholarship and other financial opportunities at CollegeBoard.com, FastWeb.com, and FinAid.

org. About 60 percent of college students actually pay less than $6,000 per year for tuition and fees. Your kids will have a lifetime to repay their student loans.

Where Should You Save the Money?

My son is about to have his second birthday and we're finally able to set aside some money for college savings. Where is the best place to do it: a 529 college-savings plan, a Coverdell education savings account, or a custodial account?

If you know you want to use the money for education, it's best to open a 529 or a Coverdell education savings account, which both provide tax-free income for education expenses.

A 529 plan is the easiest. The contribution limits are higher than you'd ever need to worry about—generally about $250,000 per beneficiary—there are no income limits to contribute, and the money grows tax free for college. You may get a state income-tax deduction for your contributions, which is available in more than half the states. (You generally need to open up a plan in your own state to qualify, although three states now let you take a deduction for contributions to any state's plan.) And you can use the money for any college in the United States and many in foreign countries. A 529 also gives you a lot of control over the money; you can switch beneficiaries to another relative if the child doesn't go to college or doesn't need the money (or if you just change your mind), and you can get your money back entirely if you decide not to use it for anyone's college, although you will owe taxes plus a 10 percent penalty on your earnings.

Coverdell education savings accounts also offer tax-free money for college as well as other educational expenses, including elementary and secondary school tuition, a computer, printer, textbooks, tutoring, educational software, and other expenses, whether your child is in public or private school. These accounts are a good choice if you want to control the investments yourself. You can open a Coverdell account at a brokerage firm or mutual fund company and you generally have the same investment choices as IRAs—often hundreds of funds and stocks. But you can only contribute up to $2,000 per beneficiary per year, which can be hard to coordinate if you and the grandparents want to contribute. And you can only contribute if your adjusted gross income is $110,000 or less if you're single, or $220,000 if filing jointly. The money must be used by age 30 or you'll owe taxes and a 10 percent penalty on the earnings.

A 2006 tax-law change made custodial accounts a much less attractive option. In the past, the first $850 of annual earnings in a custodial account was tax free and the next $850 was taxed at no more than 10 percent. Above $1,700, parents paid tax at their rate until the child turned 14. Then, the earnings were then taxed at the child's lower rate. But a 2006 tax law changed the rules. Now, those earnings on the custodial accounts are taxed at the parents' rate until your child reaches age 18. After that, the earnings are taxed at the child's rate, but the child then controls the money at age 18 or 21, depending on your state, and can use it for whatever he wants. Until the child reaches the age of majority, you control the money and can use it for anything to benefit the child, whether or not it's education related.

The custodial accounts are also in a tougher financial aid situation. The money is considered a student asset, and the federal financial aid formulas expect students to contribute 35 percent of their assets to college costs (although that number is dropping to 20 percent on July 1, 2007). On the other hand, 529s are considered to be parental assets, and parents are only expected to contribute 5.6 percent of their assets to college costs.

Both my children, ages 2 and 5, have mutual funds in custodial accounts, which I opened up soon after they were born. Should I transfer this money into 529 accounts? The 529s seem to have changed a lot over the past five years.

You ask a very timely question. The 529s have improved significantly over the past few years, and some of the biggest changes came quite recently. Two new tax laws make 529s much more attractive than custodial accounts: the 529 earnings are now permanently tax free when used for college costs, and a change in the kiddie-tax law requires parents to pay taxes on custodial account earnings at their own tax rate until the child reaches age 18 (previously, earnings had been taxed at the child's lower rate until the child turned 14). Plus, more states continue to offer income-tax deductions for 529 contributions.

And new financial aid rules give 529s a clear edge: custodial accounts are considered to be the child's assets, and children are expected to contribute 35 percent of their assets for college costs (the number shrinks to 20 percent on July 1, 2007); 529s are parental assets and only tapped at 5.6 percent in the financial aid formulas.

Because of these new rules, it's better to invest the bulk of your college savings in a 529 plan. You could also switch money from your custodial account into a 529 and benefit from future tax-free growth. The account would be a "custodial 529," which means that your children gain control when they reach the age of majority and you can't switch the beneficiary. It isn't treated as a student asset for financial aid, even though the kid controls the money.

But there's a big catch to moving the money: you can only contribute cash to a 529 account, so you'd need to sell the mutual funds and pay capital gains taxes before you can make the switch. The new kiddie-tax law makes that tricky, because the profits will be taxed at your own rate until your child turns 18 (generally 15 percent instead of 5 percent).

If your children are nearing college age, you can minimize the tax bill if you keep the money in the custodial account until age 18 and then sell the funds—especially from 2008 to 2010, when the lowest capital gains rate falls to 0 percent. If your children owe taxes on the profits, they can use the Hope or lifetime learning credit to help offset the bill. If you're worried about the impact on financial aid, wait until the junior year of college to sell the funds or take out loans and use the custodial money to pay them back soon after your child graduates.

Because your kids are younger and have only held the investments for a few years, you might not face a big tax bill on the profits—even at your own rate. In that case, it might be worthwhile to sell the funds now and pay taxes on the profits, then benefit from more than a decade of tax-free growth in the 529s.

But you don't want to switch too much money to a 529. If you pay the entire college bill with a 529, then you can't take the Hope or lifetime learning tax credit. And if you have 529 money left over after your children finish school, you'd need to switch the beneficiary or pay a 10 percent penalty (plus taxes on the gains) to access the money.

In which state's 529 plan should I invest?

Every state now offers a 529 plan, but some are much better than others. First, see if your state offers an income-tax deduction for contributing to its plan, which more than half the states offer. If it does, that's generally your best bet. New York residents, for example, can deduct up to $5,000 for single tax returns ($10,000 for joint returns) in contributions to the New York 529 plan. Virginia residents who contribute to the state's own 529 plan can deduct up to $2,000 per year per account and carry the deduction forward for an unlimited number of years if they've contributed more than that (a $6,000 contribution, for example, could get you the full $2,000 deduction for three years). Virginia's $2,000 cap on annual deductions doesn't apply to investors age 70 and older, who can deduct their full contributions in one year.

And a few states, such as Maine, Kansas, and Pennsylvania, recently started letting residents take the deduction for out-of-state 529s, too. You can look up your state's tax rules in the plan evaluator at Savingforcollege.com.

If you live in a state that doesn't offer an income-tax deduction, or one that lets you deduct contributions to any state's plan, then you'll need to assess the plans based on their fees and investment choices. Our favorite is the Iowa plan because of its low costs and variety of solid investment options, including eight Vanguard index funds. The plan also has age-weighted portfolios, which automatically adjust your investments as your child gets older. You can open an account with as little as $25 and can invest up to $239,000 per beneficiary—such a high number that few people need to worry about reaching that limit. For more information about our favorite 529s, see the college section at Kiplinger.com.

You can invest in as many different 529 accounts as you want, so you could get benefits from more than one plan. For example, you can invest enough money in your state's plan to get the maximum income-tax deduction, and if another state has better fees and investment choices, you can invest the rest of your money there, too.

Should I buy a 529 plan from a broker or directly from the state plan?

It depends on whether you're getting any extra benefit from the broker or financial advisor. When you buy an advisor-sold plan, you're typically paying an extra sales load to cover the broker's commission. But if you're doing the research and picking the plan yourself, then you can avoid the extra fees and buy the plan directly from the state on your own.

The extra commissions are not the only problem with advisor-sold 529 plans. The National Association of Securities Dealers (NASD) conducted an investigation of 20 brokerage firms and discovered that a high percentage of people who bought 529s through brokers bought out-of-state plans and hadn't always been notified of state income-tax deductions they were giving up by avoiding their own state's plan. Be very wary if a broker tries to push you into another state's plan even though your state offers an income-tax deduction for your contributions. He may be steering you in that direction just so he can earn a bigger commission. The NASD's 529 expense analyzer (available at *www.nasd.com*) can help you compare the fees for the plans you're considering.

Would you address the issue of college saving for multiple children, especially if their college careers will overlap? We have a 2-year-old and a 5-year-old and are wondering if there are any hints. Do you invest in one 529 and have one child as beneficiary for a couple of years and then switch to the younger one, or do you invest in separate plans?

Open a 529 account for each child. Even though you could lump all of your money together in one 529 in your oldest child's name, and then switch the beneficiary as each kid reaches college age, it's better to keep the accounts separate. That way, you can do a better job of matching the investments with each time frame and monitoring how close you are to your goals.

You're subject to higher gift-tax annual exclusions with multiple beneficiaries and there's no confusion about your intentions if anything happens to you. If one child doesn't go to college or needs to use less money, it's easy to switch the beneficiary to another child. And unlike custodial accounts, the 529 is considered the parents' asset for financial aid, which you're more likely to qualify for with multiple kids in school. Some states even let you take a bigger income-tax deduction each year if you invest in separate accounts.

If you don't want to worry about monitoring the investments for each account, use age-weighted funds that automatically become more conservative as each child's freshman year approaches. But be careful about 529s that charge fixed-dollar fees for each account, rather than asset-based charges.

To look up each plan's fees, tax rules, and other details, go to Savingforcollege.com.

What is the best way to save for college for my grandchildren?

Choose a 529 college-savings plan. "It's one of the most tax-favored, elderly friendly vehicles I know," says Bob Baldwin, a CPA and personal financial specialist in Charleston, South Carolina. "You can give it away but keep it. You can shelter it and not pay taxes on it."

The 529 money can be used tax free for college costs, and your contributions are tax deductible in about half the states (see Savingforcollege.com for details about each state's rules). As a grandparent, it's also a great way to get a lot of money out of your estate without worrying about gift taxes. Generally, you can only give each person $12,000 per year without being subject to gift taxes. But you're allowed to contribute five years' worth of gifts to a 529 in one year without gift taxes, totaling $60,000 per person in 2007. You may want to spread out your contributions, however, if your state limits the amount you can deduct each year.

Surprisingly, even though you can get the money out of your estate by contributing to a 529 plan, you can still maintain control over it. If one grandchild doesn't go to college, you can switch beneficiaries to another relative. Or you can take the money back entirely, if you pay a 10 percent penalty and taxes on the gains.

The contribution limits are high—generally about $250,000 per account—so you don't need to worry about coordinating with other relatives. And money in a grandparent-owned 529 generally isn't included as an asset on financial aid forms.

After your grandkids start college, you can move some more money out of your estate by paying part of their tuition bill. As long as you pay the school directly, that money isn't subject to any gift-tax limits.

How should I invest the money that I've contributed to a 529 and a Coverdell?

The good thing about a Coverdell education savings account is you get to pick the investments yourself. If you open the account at a brokerage firm, you generally have a choice of hundreds of funds and stocks. In that case, make sure that your investments match your time frame. When you have ten years or more before your kids start college, keep all of the money in a diversified portfolio of stock funds, like you would with long-term retirement savings. For specifics, see our long-term fund portfolio in the investing section of Kiplinger.com.

When your children are nearing high school, you'll want to make the portfolio a little more conservative by adding a bond fund. The Kiplinger model portfolio shifts money out of the most aggressive stock funds and moves about 30 percent of the money into a bond fund that buys all types of bonds.

As each child starts his or her junior year in high school, place enough cash in a money-market fund to cover that child's first year of college bills, so you'll know the money is there, no matter what happens to the market during that time. But you don't want to get entirely out of stock funds when your child is about to start college because you'll still have four years before the last tuition bill is due and you could benefit from the potential growth. Reallocate what's left in the child's account so 30 percent to 40 percent of the assets are in bond funds, with the rest in stock funds until your child is almost finished with college. Repeat the same step every year until all the assets are in a money-market fund.

Your investment choices are a lot easier for a 529. Most only have a handful of funds from which to choose; you can put together a diversified portfolio of the stock-fund choices for the early years and gradually get more conservative through time (moving some money into the bond funds and fixed accounts). If you don't want to worry about monitoring the investments, most 529s let you invest in age-weighted funds—like target-retirement funds—that invest in a portfolio of funds to match your timeframe and gradually become more conservative as the tuition bill gets closer. Each plan's age-weighted funds are constructed a bit differently, so make sure that the one you choose doesn't become too conservative too quickly.

If a minor child has a custodial account set up in CDs, what advantage is gained if they are rolled over into a 529 account? The amount is currently $30,000 in CDs and $10,000 in a money market, and we plan to use it for college costs in the next few years.

There are two good reasons to roll the money from a custodial account into a 529: taxes and financial aid. Depending on how much he earns, your child could be paying taxes on his CD interest every year. And because of a recent tax law change, earnings on custodial account money are now taxed at the parents' rate until age 18. In the past, custodial account money had been taxed at the parents' rate only until the child turned age 14, and then it was taxed at the child's lower rate. Move the money into a 529 account and you will avoid the tax bill in the future.

You can only invest cash in a 529, so you'd have to sell the investments before making the switch. That would trigger a capital gains tax bill for money that had been invested in stocks or mutual funds, but you don't need to worry about that tax bill either because the money was in CDs and a money-market account.

Regarding financial aid, the federal formula requires parents to contribute just 5.6 percent of their assets to the college costs, but students have to contribute 35 percent of their assets (the number shrinks to 20 percent on July 1, 2007). Custodial account money is considered the child's assets, but money in a 529 plan is considered a parental asset—even if it had been transferred from a custodial account. Because it's a custodial arrangement, though, the money still technically belongs to your child, who can control how it's used when he or she reaches the age of majority (18 or 21, depending on the state), and you can't change the beneficiary, like you could with other 529 accounts.

I am 24 years old and single, but I hope to have a family someday. Can I open a 529 college-savings account even though I don't have children? I am always thinking ahead and would love to get started.

Congratulations on your foresight and, yes, you can take advantage of a tax-sheltered 529 plan now. Just name yourself the beneficiary; you can change the designation to a child at a later date. You'll generally be able to take a state income-tax deduction if it's available in your state, even though you're currently making contributions for yourself.

If you never have kids on which to spend the money, you can use it for your own education or switch the beneficiary to another family member—your wife, perhaps, or even a cousin.

One of the vehicles I've used for saving for college is U.S. savings bonds. Over time, my income level has approached the limit at which I would no longer receive the advertised tax-free benefits if used for college. I started buying the bonds because of the very advantage I will now be losing. Is there any way that I can still realize the benefit or roll the funds into another vehicle and maintain the benefit?

That's the tough thing about using savings bonds for college: the interest is only tax free for college tuition if your adjusted gross income is below $128,400 if married, $80,600 if single in 2007. (The amount you can exclude from taxes starts to phase out for married couples earning more than $98,400 or singles earning more than $65,600.) That number, which also includes the value of the bonds you cash out, increases a bit with inflation each year.

Also keep in mind that the tax break only applies to series EE bonds issued after 1989 or series I bonds, and you need to be at least 24 years old on the bond's issue date (bonds in the child's name don't count). You can only get the tax break for college tuition and fees, not room and board.

There is one way to get out, though, if you think your income will pass the cutoff by the time your child goes to college: you can make a tax-free switch from savings bonds to a 529 college-savings account, which will let you use the money tax free for college costs no matter how much money you earn when you finally spend the money. But you can only make the switch in a year when your income falls below the cutoff for the savings bond tax break. So it's a good idea to move the money now if your income is increasing each year but hasn't yet reached the limit, or in a year when you have an unusually low income, such as if one parent was unemployed or stayed home with the kids.

I have some EE savings bonds that qualify for my son's college tuition payments without being taxed. Are they tax free for graduate school, too?

Maybe, but only in very specific circumstances. The savings bond interest is only tax free for college tuition if your adjusted gross income is below $128,400 if married, $80,600 if single in 2007. The bond owner has to be at least 24 years old when the bond was first issued—which means that undergraduate students usually can't get the tax break for bonds in their own name—and the money must be used for tuition and fees (room and board doesn't count).

Graduate school tuition is considered a qualified educational expense, but there could be a catch: the bond must be used for the bond owner, spouse, or a dependent whom you claim as an exemption on your return. If your child is no longer considered your dependent for tax purposes, then you can't get the savings bond tax break to help pay their grad school tuition.

As long as you bought the bonds when you were 24 or older and still qualify under the income limits, you can use bonds you own for your own tuition if you go back to school, however. And adult children could even buy bonds themselves at age 24 or older and use them tax-free for their own grad school costs in the future.

My grandmother bought three savings bonds for my family and one for my son before she died, but we don't have any information about them. How can I find out where they are?

The Bureau of the Public Debt can help you track them down. Write the bureau a letter listing the names and Social Security numbers of the family members for whom you believe the bonds were purchased (along with your grandmother's name and Social Security number, if you believe she was a co-owner). Include the approximate date on which your grandmother made the purchase, or at least a range of years. Also include any additional information you may have, such as the bond series (EE, I) and denomination.

Send the letter to the Bureau of the Public Debt, P.O. Box 1328, Parkersburg, West Virgina 26106-1328. It can also help to fill out form 1048 at the Bureau's Web site (*www.treasurydirect.gov*) if you have enough information to answer most of the questions there.

If you know all the details about the bonds, including serial numbers, the bureau can generally track them down and have them reissued within three to four weeks. Otherwise, the search could take months.

If the bonds were in your grandmother's name, rather than your family's name, you'll also need to prove that you're entitled to the money.

I'm interested in investing in a prepaid tuition plan for my daughter, but I remember that several states' plans closed a few years ago or changed their calculations. Are these still as good a deal as they had been in the past?

Prepaid tuition plans were always an interesting concept: you'd pay for tomorrow's college costs at today's prices. It was a way to put down a chunk of money to cover part of the cost of college, and avoid the future price hikes that came with inflation. With the cost of college increasing by about 5 percent per year, the prepaid plans were a great complement to 529s, which provided the potential for greater returns over the long run, but also had more risk for the investor.

But then prepaid tuition plans started to become *too* good a deal. The average tuition at four-year public colleges has increased by at least 7 percent in every year since 2001, peaking with an average price hike of 13 percent in 2003—with increases much higher in some states. This greatly benefitted the families who already owned the prepaid tuition plans, especially as the stock market and interest rates dwindled during that time.

But the prepaid plans put the states that offered them in a tough situation. During those same years, many states had a tough time investing their own money to guarantee that they'd have enough cash to cover those costs. As a result several states, such as Ohio, closed their plans until the tuition increases settled down, and other states added a premium to their prices. Now, investors in many states have to pay for today's tuition plus a 5 percent to 20 percent premium, making them not quite as good a deal as they had been in the past.

Depending on the size of the premium, however, prepaid tuition plans can still be a good way to diversify your college savings while investing the rest of your long-term savings in a 529, if you still have several years before your child attends college. (If your child is just a few years away from college, the tuition may not increase enough in that short time to make up for an extra premium you may have to pay for a prepaid plan.)

Find out about the plan's rules if your child doesn't attend a public college in your state. Also check out the state's guarantees. Many guarantee that they will cover the full tuition as promised, even if the plan has an investing shortfall. Others have more flexibility to make changes to your contract after you've already invested your money.

A recent financial aid change helped all kinds of prepaid tuition plans. In the past, money in these plans was considered to be the student's assets and tapped at 35 percent to pay for college costs (the number will fall to 20 percent on July 1, 2007). But now they're considered to be parents' assets and they are tapped at just 5.6 percent in the financial aid formulas, just like all 529 plans.

My son was born in December, and I'm considering an Independent 529 plan, a prepaid tuition plan that includes Notre Dame. But I understand that if he does not go there, the amount refunded to me will include a mere 2 percent annual return. Is this a bad deal?

The Independent 529 plan lets you pay tomorrow's tuition (or part of it) at today's prices for hundreds of private colleges, including many big name schools such as Notre Dame, Princeton, Emory, the University of Chicago, Stanford, Amherst, Tulane, Wake Forest, and Wellesley. The number of participating schools continues to increase. For a full list, see the Independent 529 Plan Web site (*www.independent529plan.com*).

The value of your contribution depends on the current cost of each college. If you contribute $10,000 now, for example, you'll get a tuition certificate that covers one year of full tuition at a college that currently costs $10,000 annually, or one-third of one year's tuition bill at a school that currently costs $30,000. As an added bonus, all of the schools are offering tuition discounts of at least 0.5 percent for Independent 529 plan participants.

Prepaying college costs can be valuable considering that the average tuition and fees at four-year private colleges increased by 5.9 percent in the past year, according to the College Board. The Independent 529 money is tax free if used to pay college bills, and you're guaranteed to have a set portion of the tuition bill paid off no matter what happens to the cost of college or the stock market in the future.

But you're right about the downside. If you don't use the money at one of the participating schools (if your son ends up going to Harvard, Yale, Duke, Northwestern University, or a state college, for example), then the account will only be worth the original investment plus returns of up to 2 percent per year. You could roll over your Independent 529 plan money into a regular 529 account at any time, but your returns until that point will be limited to the 2 percent per year. Or you could switch the beneficiary to another family member who may attend a participating school.

If you worry that your child won't end up at one of the schools on the list, then you might be better off investing in a traditional 529 state college savings plan. Your return will depend on the plan's mutual fund investments, and the money can be used at any college, public or private.

If Grandma contributed money to a 529 plan and then after separation/divorce of the parents withdrew the money prior to the child's 18th birthday, can the child contest the withdrawal in court?

You'd generally have a tough time getting the money. In most cases, the owner of the 529 account can change the beneficiary to another relative without any trouble. In fact, that's one of the big attractions for grandparents, who can switch the 529 to another grandchild if one gets a full scholarship or doesn't end up going to college—or for any reason.

You can make the change without any income-tax consequences as long as the new beneficiary is a member of the original beneficiary's family, including their child, brother, sister, stepbrother or stepsister, father or mother, stepfather or stepmother, son-in-law, daughter-in-law, father-in-law, mother-in-law, brother-in-law or sister-in-law, the spouse of any of those people, or a first cousin (enabling Grandma to switch the money to another grandchild who isn't a brother or sister).

And if Grandma doesn't mind paying taxes and penalties, she can even take the money back for herself. The one exception is if the money had originally been in a custodial account for the child and then was rolled over into a 529. In that case, it is legally the child's money and you can take Grandma to court to try to get it back.

Can I use money from my Roth IRA for college costs?

Yes you can, but there are many better options. You can withdraw the contributions from your Roth IRA at any time without a penalty or tax bill. And you can withdraw your earnings penalty free for college expenses, although you will have to pay taxes on your earnings.

That tax bill is definitely a drawback. But the biggest downside to tapping the Roth IRA money is that you can't ever put it back, costing you years of tax-free growth. You can only invest up to $4,000 into a Roth IRA in 2007 ($5,000 if you're 50 or older), so there is a big limit on the amount of money you can have in the account for retirement.

Say, for example, you withdrew $15,000 from your Roth IRA at age 45 for college costs. You may or may not have a tax bill, depending on how much money you'd contributed to the account. But you will have the opportunity cost. If you'd kept that money in the account for 20 more years instead and your investments averaged 8 percent per year, you could have amassed nearly $70,000 in tax-free money by the time you retire, rather than the $15,000 you'd take for college costs now.

It's a much better idea to save college money in a 529 college-savings fund instead, which will give you tax-free money for college and let you keep your retirement money in the IRA for your future expenses.

How to Master Financial Aid

Is it better to have funds intended to be used for college and college expenses in the parents' name or the child's name?

Both the tax laws and financial aid rules changed recently to make saving for college in a custodial account in your child's name not nearly as good a deal as it had been in the past.

Until recently, money invested for your children in a custodial account—either a Uniform Gifts to Minors Act (UGMA) or Uniform Transfers to Minors Act (UTMA)—was taxed at a very low rate. The first $850 of annual earnings was tax-free, and the next $850 was taxed at no more than 10 percent, and for amounts above $1,700, parents paid tax at their rate until the child turned 14. At that point, earnings were taxed at the child's lower rate. Those rules recently changed. Now, the earnings on the custodial account are taxed at the parents' rate until the child reaches age 18, not 14. If you do have custodial account money, it's a good idea to avoid tapping the account until after your kid starts college.

But at that point, there can be a control issue. The plus side is that you can use the money for anything to benefit the child until he reaches the age of majority, either 18 or 21, depending on your state. At that point, however, the child takes over the account and hopefully uses it to pay for college, not a fancy car.

And there's a big financial aid hit. Students are expected to contribute 35 percent of their assets for college costs (the number will shrink to 20 percent on July 1, 2007). But parents are only expected to contribute 5.6 percent of their assets for college. Parental assets include money they've saved in their own name, but it also includes 529 accounts. So with 529s, you now get a double benefit: the money is totally tax free if used for college costs and it's considered a parental asset, so it's only tapped at 5.6 percent for financial aid purposes.

You can switch money from a custodial account into a 529, which could be a good move to make before your child's junior year of high school if you'd like to improve your financial aid situation, but you can only invest cash in a 529 so you'd have to sell the stocks or funds and pay income taxes on the earnings at your child's rate. But it could still be worthwhile depending on the size of the tax bill if it makes a big difference in your financial aid situation. And future earnings within the 529 won't be taxed at all.

Money that had been in a custodial account, however, has special rules even after it's been shifted to a 529. Because it is your kid's money, you can't change the beneficiary from a custodial 529 (unlike regular 529s) and your child will still control the money after he reaches age 18 or 21.

My son will be starting college in a few years and I think I earn too much to qualify for financial aid. Is it still worthwhile to file the financial aid forms?

I t's definitely worthwhile to submit the forms. According to the College Board, almost $135 billion in financial aid was distributed in the 2005–2006 school year. The average full-time student received $5,144 in federal loans and $4,433 in grants.

Some pricey private schools give out more money than you might expect. For example, 93 percent of students in the class of 2008 at Princeton who applied for financial aid and whose families earned between $120,000 and $139,999 a year were eligible for aid. The average grant was $14,000 (grants are higher for families who earn less).

To see if you qualify for need-based aid, run your numbers through the expected family contribution calculator at Finaid.org. You'll get an estimate of how much your family will be expected to pay for college expenses.

And find out if your state offers money for students with high grade-point averages or standardized test scores. Georgia residents who earn at least a 3.0 grade-point average in high school and college qualify for free tuition at Georgia state colleges or a $3,000 discount at private schools in the state. Louisiana, Massachusetts, Nevada, New Mexico, and several other states offer sizable scholarships to residents who attend state colleges and had good grades or scores.

I read that the University of Pennsylvania just started offering free tuition and room and board for low-income families. Do any other colleges have similar programs?

P enn joins a handful of big-name public and private colleges offering special deals for families whose incomes fall below certain levels. At Penn, the limit is much higher than you might expect; the program is available to families with annual incomes of $50,000 or less.

Financial aid always helped low-income families afford the giant college bills—Penn's list-price tuition is $32,400 and room and board is $9,400 for the current school year—but the new program's key feature is that it promises to meet the family's entire need with no loans. The highest-need students received grant aid of more than $45,000 in the 2006–2007 school year.

There's been a lot of competitive activity in this area over the past year. Stanford introduced a similar program for students whose families earn less than $45,000. Harvard, which started its program in 2004, raised the income limit from $40,000 to $60,000 and reduced contributions for families earning up to $80,000. MIT said it would match Federal Pell Grants with its own grant program, covering a big part of the costs for families earning less than $40,000. Yale announced that families earning less than $45,000 would get a free ride, with substantial cuts in the contribution required for families earning up to $60,000. And in 2001, Princeton replaced student loans in the financial aid package with grants for all students.

Several public colleges, such as the University of North Carolina at Chapel Hill, the University of Virginia, and the University of Maryland also have similar programs.

These programs make it worthwhile to apply to some high-priced schools even if you don't think you have enough money to pay the bills. But there's one big catch: you need to get accepted into the college, which can be tough to do. Harvard only accepted 9.1 percent of its applicants for last year's freshman class. Still, it can be worth a try and generally just requires the standard aid application.

Do those scholarship programs look at just income, or income as well as assets?

The colleges generally consider income first, but then also look at assets so rich people without regular jobs don't try to cheat the system. Harvard, for example, counts taxable as well as nontaxed income, and then considers assets on a case-by-case basis, including home equity and retirement and other savings. The University of North Carolina at Chapel Hill uses adjusted gross income as the first test (200 percent of the poverty level, which is about $37,000), and then looks at assets such as home equity and savings.

Even though the actual calculations are more complex, the schools started publicizing the income limits as a way to let people know that the financial aid is available. Most of these colleges always provided generous financial aid—about 50 percent of Harvard's students receive some need-based grant aid, for example—but many people didn't realize how much help they could get. "We needed to speak about our financial aid program in a simple, clear way in order to recruit talented students from low-income families who weren't applying because they didn't think the aid was available," says Sally Donahue, director of financial aid at Harvard.

Don't worry too much about the specific limits. You don't need to apply separately for these programs—you just need to submit the standard aid forms—and you may get a hefty aid package even if you don't get the full ride. About 1,000 families earning $100,000 or more still get need-based grant aid at Harvard, says Donahue. UNC-Chapel Hill meets 100 percent of families' need for everyone; it's just that families with more money might have more loans in their financial aid packages.

I'm divorced and my son is in high school right now. Because I share custody with my ex-husband, which one of us will need to fill out the financial aid forms? Will my current husband's finances be included, too?

Only the custodial parent's finances are considered for federal aid and most state aid. If you share custody, the parent with whom the student lived the longest over the past year must submit the information. If the student lived with each parent equally, then the parent who provided more than half the child's support over the past year must submit the information.

If that parent has remarried, the stepparent's finances are included, too. So if you're considered the custodial parent and have provided the most support, you'll need to fill out the federal aid forms with information from yourself and your current husband.

Even if you are not considered the custodial parent, however, you may still need to submit financial information to some private colleges.

For more details about the rules for divorce and financial aid, including information about college support agreements, see FinAid.com's Divorce and Financial Aid page.

Is it worthwhile to sign up for a service that offers to search for scholarships? I hear that some of them are scams.

You're right; some of these services are scams, and you usually don't get much out of the paid services that you couldn't do on your own for free.

First, ask your child's high school guidance counselor about scholarships and talk with the schools you're considering about their special programs. Also find out about any scholarship opportunities available from your employer or any professional organizations in the field that your child will be studying.

Then check out several Web sites that provide free scholarship search services, such as FastWeb.com, CollegeBoard.com, Petersons.com, and Collegeanswer .com. You'll type in a lot of information about your child and your family, such as major, religion, ethnic background, special talents, parents' employers, and clubs. Then the services list details about each of the scholarships for which your child may qualify. It may take a lot of legwork to submit the applications, but the free money you could get makes it worthwhile.

Finaid.org also has a good list of other financial aid resources, such as information about military scholarships and other special programs.

Strategies for Withdrawing the Money

I have money in several different accounts to pay for my children's college. Most of it is in a 529 plan, but some is in a Coverdell education savings account and some is in a custodial account. Which should I use first to pay college bills?

Taxes are the deciding factor. First determine whether you qualify for the Hope or lifetime learning tax credit. If so, don't pay the full tuition bill from a 529 or a Coverdell account. College withdrawals from those accounts are already tax free, and you're not permitted to double up on tax breaks.

You're eligible for the Hope credit if your adjusted gross income in 2007 is less than $94,000 on a joint return (or $47,000 if you're single). In that case, you get a tax credit of up to $1,650 per child in each child's first two years of college (the credit amount phases out entirely if you earn more than $114,000 if married filing jointly, or $57,000 if single). In order to claim the credit, however, you have to pay at least $2,200 of your bill from an account other than a 529 or a Coverdell. So it makes sense to tap your custodial account.

After your child's first two years of college, you may qualify for the lifetime learning credit of up to $2,000 per tax return. You have to meet the same income requirements as for the Hope credit, plus you have to pay at least $10,000 in college bills from a source other than a 529 or a Coverdell.

Save Money on Insurance

Chapter 3

People tend to underestimate the importance of insurance. It's essential to protect your financial plan, and knowing some smart shopping strategies can be one of the easiest ways to free up hundreds—even thousands—of dollars from your budget.

But people tend to make big mistakes when it comes to insurance because they don't like to think about the topic. They end up paying too much money for products they may not even need and don't know about simple strategies that can cut their costs. Or they buy the wrong kind of coverage and lack protection they think they have. I get questions from so many people who know how important insurance can be, but have no idea how to get started or who to trust.

I love answering those questions. I've been writing about insurance for more than 15 years and know about all the tricks for dealing with the business—whether it's avoiding agents who are just trying to earn a big commission, moves people make that inadvertently get them dropped by their homeowners' insurance company, and little-known information such as the semi-secret database where insurers share claims information about you and how big a difference your credit score can make in your auto insurance rate. I also know some simple strategies that can help you cut your premiums in half if you have a teenage driver, lower your costs significantly if you're buying long-term care insurance, save a lot of money on health insurance, and calculate how much life and homeowners' insurance you need—two numbers that most people tend to get wrong.

If you know what you're doing, you can save a lot of money on insurance premiums and make sure you have the right coverage, so you can spend a lot less time worrying about possible events that could ruin your financial plans.

Health Insurance

My employer offers several health insurance choices during open enrollment period. How do I pick the best one for my family?

Employers have been struggling with the high cost of health insurance over the past few years and have been making big changes to their employees' coverage and costs. It's a good idea for everyone to review all of their employer's options during open enrollment season, even if you've been with the same plan for a long time. Because of the changes, the plan you chose a few years ago may no longer be the best option for your family.

The changes aren't always obvious. Employers have been increasing their employees' share of the premiums—and boosting the cost of family coverage even more—but they've also been charging more in co-payments, deductibles, and other expenses. Some now offer tiered coverage for hospital stays and prescription drugs, charging you a lot more for services that aren't on a preferred list. They've also been charging more for every doctor's visit and increasing out-of-pocket coverage caps, leaving you with thousands of dollars in extra expenses if you have a major medical condition.

Because of these extra costs, the policy with the lowest premium may actually end up costing you the most by the end of the year.

Meanwhile, many employers are offering new options, such as high-deductible health insurance plans paired with a tax-deductible health savings account (HSA), which could be a great deal if premiums are low and the employer contributes to the savings plan.

To compare policies, you need to run the numbers for your typical health care expenses for the year and calculate how much you'd end up paying out of your pocket. Also compare the amount you'd owe for catastrophic care. Many employers offer calculators to help you run the numbers.

Go through all of your options, as well as any coverage through your spouse's employer. As a way to cut down on their own costs, many employers started boosting premiums significantly for family coverage. Even if your spouse and kids had been on your policy in the past, your spouse's policy may be a better deal for the family now. And some employers have been giving bonuses to people who turn down the employer's health insurance, which could make it worthwhile for all of you to switch to your spouse's plan.

I just found out that the premiums for health insurance through my employer are going to jump a lot next year and the coverage isn't that great. Do you think I might find a better deal if I drop my employer's coverage and buy my own policy?

Prices for employee health insurance have increased significantly over the past few years, with the total premiums rising by 87 percent since 2000, according to the Kaiser Family Foundation. The average family plan cost $11,480 per year, or $4,242 for singles in 2006.

But employee coverage has two big benefits you can't get with an individual plan: you generally can't get rejected because of your health, and most employers continue to subsidize a big chunk of the costs, covering 73 percent of the bill for family coverage, and 84 percent for singles. The average worker only pays $627 of the bill per year for single coverage, or $2,973 for the average family.

Individual insurance is generally less expensive than the total cost of employee coverage, if you're healthy and live in a state with a competitive health insurance marketplace (which includes most states other than New York, New Jersey, and Massachusetts, which have very high individual health insurance prices). But if your employer has been subsidizing a big chunk of the bill, it may be tougher to find a better deal on your own. Many employers are having a tough time covering the costs themselves, however, and are shifting a much bigger share of the premium to their employees, so it wouldn't hurt to compare your options.

To see what you could get on your own, you can shop for individual health insurance policies from several companies at eHealthInsurance.com. Or for personalized attention, you can find a health insurance agent in your area through the National Association of Health Underwriters (*www.nahu.org*). You can also find a list of companies offering health insurance in your area through your state insurance department (see *www*
.naic.org for links to your state regulator).

If you are looking at individual plans, also make sure you're getting all the coverage you need; these plans may have exclusions and coverage limits that are very different than your employer's plan. Compare total out-of-pocket costs for your expected medical expenses for the year—and any caps on catastrophic costs—rather than just looking at premiums. Employers have been raising rates for dependents a lot more than for employees, so also compare prices for staying on the policy yourself while buying a separate policy for your family.

And keep in mind that the price will be a lot higher for the individual plan if you have any medical conditions. Never drop your group policy before guaranteeing that you have coverage elsewhere, just in case it ends up being tougher to get the new policy than you were expecting.

One of the best ways to lower your premiums is to increase your deductible, which will also help you qualify to open a health savings account that lets you make tax-deductible contributions of up to $2,850 for individual coverage and $5,650 for families in 2007 and gives you a stash of money to use tax-free for medical expenses in any year.

What do I have to do to qualify for a health savings account? Where's the best place to keep the HSA money?

You can have a health savings account either through your employer or if you have an individual policy. To qualify, you must have an HSA-eligible high-deductible health insurance policy, which means a deductible of at least $1,100 for individual coverage, $2,200 for families in 2007, and you must meet a few other requirements. (Ask your insurer if your policy qualifies.)

Then, you can open a health savings account and contribute up to $2,850 for individual coverage, $5,650 for families in 2007 (people age 55 or older can make an extra catch-up contribution of $800 in 2007). Your contributions are tax deductible and you can use the money tax free for medical expenses in any year. Money you don't use that year can remain in the account for future expenses. After age 65, you can use the money penalty free for anything, although you'll have to pay taxes on your earnings for nonmedical expenses.

Many insurers offer HSAs paired with their high-deductible policies, but you don't have to go with that account. Look for an account with low fees and good investment choices. Some only offer a savings account offering 3 percent to 4 percent interest, but others let you invest in mutual funds. That's a better option if you plan on keeping the money in the account for a long time, using other cash for your current medical expenses so you can keep more money in the HSA for future expenses and make the most of the tax-free growth.

You can find lists of companies offering HSA-eligible policies at HSAInsider.com (*www.hsainsider.com*), HealthDecisions.org (*www.healthdecisions.org/hsa*), or eHealthInsurance.com (*www.ehealthinsurance.com*). If you find better investing choices elsewhere, you can switch HSA administrators, rolling the money over directly to another account so you don't get a tax hit, much like you would with an IRA.

If your employer offers you an HSA account option that has decent investment choices, you aren't required to open the account with that administrator, but it might be your best choice; it's usually a lot easier to have your contributions automatically deducted from your paycheck and your employer may cover some of the administrative costs.

I don't have health insurance through work and I've been thinking about increasing my deductible so I can open a health savings account. What type of calculations should I do to figure out whether this would be a good move for me?

If you're already buying insurance on your own, it's generally a good move to increase your deductible. You'll need to compare the premium savings you'd get by raising your deductible to the extra out-of-pocket costs you could incur, and you'll also need to factor in the tax savings you'll get from the HSA.

The following example from eHealthInsurance.com shows how much a typical family could save by switching to an HSA. A San Diego couple in their mid-30s with two kids would pay about $9,936 per year in premiums for a health insurance policy with a $500 deductible. If they raised their deductible to $4,800, they could lower their annual premiums to $2,712—a $7,224 savings. They could then set aside $4,800 in their HSA to cover the full deductible and still have $2,424 in extra cash left over. If they were in the 25 percent federal and 9 percent state tax bracket, they'd lower their tax bill by $1,632 per year by contributing to the HSA.

Then, say they only used $2,000 from their HSA for medical expenses each year, leaving an extra $2,800 in the account to grow. If that continued for the next 30 years and the money was invested at just 4 percent, they'd have more than $160,000 at retirement. Any money they used for medical expenses would be tax free.

You can get an even bigger bang from the HSA if you can afford to pay your out-of-pocket medical expenses from other money and leave the HSA account to grow tax deferred for decades. If you finally use the money on medical expenses after retirement, you can access the stash years later tax free, giving it even greater tax advantages than a 401(k) or traditional IRA. If you're investing for the long run and plan to use other money for current medical costs, then it's best to find an HSA that lets you invest in stock funds, not just a fixed account.

Go to HSAInsider.com for a list of insurance companies offering high-deductible policies and administrators offering the savings accounts. You can get price quotes from several HSA-eligible policies in most states at eHealthInsurance.com, then run your numbers through their calculator to see how the tax benefits and long-term savings could add up in your own situation. HSAfinder.com (*www.hsafinder.com*) also helps you find many HSA administrators; and HealthDecisions.org can help you find HSA-eligible health insurance policies.

I'm about to leave my job at a big company that offers great benefits and plan to start my own business. But I'm worried about my health insurance. I've had great coverage through my employer but I don't know what I should do when I go off on my own. Any advice?

If your spouse has an employee policy on which you can get coverage, that's usually your best bet. But that isn't an option for many people.

As long as your previous employer had 20 or more employees, you can continue on your old group policy for up to 18 months after you leave your job under a federal law called COBRA. But be prepared for sticker shock. You'll have to pay 100 percent of the premiums yourself, plus up to 2 percent in administrative charges. This can be a huge surprise if your employer had covered part of the bill, which many of them do. In 2006, the average employee paid $2,973 for family coverage, while employers kicked in $8,508, according to the Kaiser Family Foundation. With COBRA, you'd be footing the whole bill yourself, averaging $11,480 for family coverage in 2006.

If you're in poor health, this still could be your best bet because you can't be rejected for any medical conditions. If you're healthy, though, you may get a better deal on your own. Check out price quotes for individual policies at eHealthInsurance.com or contact a health insurance agent for help. You can go to the National Association of Health Underwriters Web site (*www.nahu.org*)—the organization for health insurance agents—to find an agent in your area. Self-employed people can deduct 100 percent of their premiums from their taxes if they aren't eligible for coverage through an employer.

Keep in mind that the prices can vary tremendously by state depending on the laws for individual health insurance coverage. Most states let insurers charge higher premiums for people in poor health, which means you'll get a good deal if you're healthy. Other states, such as New York and New Jersey, require insurers to charge everyone the same rate, regardless of their age or health. People in poor health can get a relatively good deal there, but young healthy people end up paying a lot more than they would in other states.

Another way to save money: buy a high-deductible health insurance policy and open a health savings account. Raising your deductible will lower your premium, and the HSA contributions are tax deductible and can grow tax free for future medical expenses.

I left my job to start a freelance business almost a year and a half ago and stayed on my former employer's health insurance plan through COBRA. But now that my COBRA coverage is about to expire, I'm shopping around for health insurance on my own and have already been turned down by three companies because I have a blood disease. What should I do?

Contact a health insurance agent in your area who knows from experience which companies are likely to insure people with your conditions. You can find one through the National Association of Health Underwriters Web site (*www.nahu.org*) or call eHealthInsurance.com at 800-977-8860, which works with many companies. (If you have medical conditions, it's better to call them than to get price quotes online.) Tell the agent all the details about your health and see if they know of any companies that are likely to insure you.

Each insurer treats medical problems very differently. Some companies may reject a person, while others may offer them the policy but increase their rate (often by 25 percent to 300 percent above the price for healthy people) or exclude certain conditions from coverage. You can also get a lot of helpful information about which insurers sell policies in your area from your state insurance department Web site (see *www.naic.org* for links).

If you can't find coverage through a regular company, you may be able to get insurance through your state's high-risk health insurance pool if you live in one of the 33 states that offers that option. The rules vary significantly from state to state. In some states, you must first be turned down by one or two insurance companies, which is already the case for you; in others you can only sign up for the pool's coverage during one particular open enrollment period during the year. The price is usually capped at 125 percent to 150 percent higher than the price of a standard policy, depending on state rules.

To find out if your state has a health insurance pool, see the National Association of State Comprehensive Health Insurance Plans Web site (*www.naschip.org*). Communicating for Agriculture and the Self-Employed, a nonprofit group that produces a comprehensive guide to high-risk coverage, also has a high-risk pool site (*www .selfemployedcountry.org/riskpools.html*).

A few states, however, don't have high-risk pools. In some, such as New York and New Jersey, insurance companies must cover everyone regardless of their health; obviously, you don't live in one of those states. In others, such as Nevada and Arizona, there is no pool. Florida technically has a pool, but it hasn't been offering policies for more than ten years so it essentially has no open pool, which means that some people won't be able to get insurance at any price. This is an important point to consider if you're about to retire to one of the states without a pool before you're eligible for Medicare at age 65.

Some of these states, however, do offer some consumer protections; for example, in Florida, many insurers must offer you a continuation policy after COBRA expires, as long as your previous policy made you eligible and you haven't gone without coverage for more than 63 days. The rules are complicated and vary a lot from state to state; contact your state insurance department for more information about any consumer protections that might help you, and make sure you understand the rules before dropping any coverage, which could make you ineligible for some of the continuation policies. For this reason, it's a good idea to start shopping for an individual policy several months before your COBRA coverage expires.

My daughter is about to graduate from college this spring and still hasn't found a job. I'm starting to get worried about her health insurance. She loses coverage under our policy soon after she graduates. What can we do?

Many families go through the same situation, because most health insurance policies provided by employers cover kids only while they're full-time students, up to age 25 (and coverage stops when they leave school, even if they're younger than that). But there are several ways to insure your daughter after she graduates.

Even though you won't be able to keep your daughter on your policy as a dependent after she graduates, she may still be able to continue that coverage under COBRA, a federal law that lets you stay in a group plan for up to 36 months after you no longer qualify for coverage as a dependent. (This is the same law that requires most employers to let you continue coverage for up to 18 months after you leave your job.) These policies are generally a lot more expensive than individual policies if you're healthy—especially because your employer is no longer subsidizing part of the premiums—but insurers cannot reject you because of your health.

It's a good idea to sign up for COBRA coverage at first, even if you're healthy, so you know you have some coverage if you end up getting rejected for other policies. People with relatively minor medical conditions can still have a tough time finding affordable individual coverage, which can come as quite a surprise when they finally shop around. Make sure you at least have this safety net before you shop around for other coverage; you can always drop it after you get approved for a better alternative.

If your daughter is healthy and it looks like she'll be without health insurance for a while, check out prices for regular individual health insurance policies, which can be a lot less expensive than COBRA if she doesn't have any medical conditions. A 22-year-old woman in Grand Rapids could get an individual policy through eHealthInsurance.com for just $48 per month with a $1,000 deductible. (The cost varies by city and sex; a 22-year-old male in Chicago would pay about $94 monthly for a policy with a $1,000 deductible.)

Getting a high-deductible individual policy also gives you an added bonus: you'll save money on premiums and you may be able to open up a health savings account. You can make tax-deductible contributions to the HSA and use the money tax free to pay your deductible and other medical expenses. And if you end up having few medical expenses, an HSA can be a wonderful savings tool; money you don't use that year can grow in the account tax free for future medical costs or build up into a tax-deferred retirement fund.

And if it looks like she'll be getting health coverage through work in the next few months, a short-term policy is another inexpensive option. A 22-year-old woman in Grand Rapids would pay about $60 per month for an Assurant Health short-term policy with a 20 percent co-pay and a $1,000 deductible ($45 a month with a $2,500 deductible). You can use the policy with any doctor or hospital. For price quotes, check with Assurant Health (*www.temporaryinsurance.com*) or Golden Rule (*www.goldenrule.com*), two large national companies providing short-term coverage. You can also find short-term coverage through eHealthInsurance.com, which sells several companies' policies.

Homeowners' Insurance

I put in a claim on my homeowners' insurance about three years ago for a $1,200 leak caused by wind. Now, I had a pipe burst in my wall. It caused damage to the ceiling below the leak and there is water under my bathroom tile floor. I may have to remove the tiles. I had to rent fans and a dehumidifier, which was expensive. I was thinking of just paying for it all, but isn't that what homeowners' insurance is for? The result of the damage is adding up quickly. If I put in a claim, I have heard that I could get dropped or have to pay high rates. What do you suggest? If you have a legitimate claim, should you eat the cost or put in the claim?

It depends on the size of the claim and your deductible. Submitting a claim that only pays a few hundred dollars after your deductible could end up costing you a lot more in the long run—especially because this is your second water-damage claim. Insurance companies are particularly worried about small water-damage claims that could end up growing into very expensive mold problems. They pay out the legitimate claims, but are much more likely to drop those customers when their policies are up for renewal.

In a study by the California Insurance Department, 25 percent of the companies refused to renew the policies of customers who made one or two non-water-damage claims in the past three years. And 32 percent refused to renew policies for people who made one or two water loss claims in the past three years.

You're right that this seems strange to avoid submitting legitimate claims when you actually have insurance. But these are the new rules of homeowners' insurance.

A few years ago, many homeowners' insurance companies made an effort to become more profitable and decided they didn't want to deal with people who submitted small claims. The administrative costs were big even if the payouts were small, and they also worried that small claims could lead to much larger ones, such as very expensive mold claims that could arise from water damage. That's why you need to be particularly careful in your situation.

And getting dropped by your insurance company isn't the only problem. Insurers share claims information with each other through a database called the Comprehensive Loss Underwriting Exchange (CLUE), and other insurers may not want to insure you after you've had a few small claims either, even if they were with another insurance company. In the California Insurance Department study, 62 percent of the top 13 companies refused applicants with only one or two claims in the past three years.

If you do find an insurer to cover you, you may end up paying a lot more for the coverage than you had in the past. I've talked with way too many people who submitted claims that paid out just $200 or $300 after their deductible and then were dropped by their insurer and ended up having to pay double the premiums with a new insurance company, costing them much more than $200 or $300 extra in premiums over the next year or two.

Because these are the new rules of the game, it's best to adjust your game plan too. If you aren't going to submit small claims, then you shouldn't have to pay for insurance you aren't going to use. The best move is to increase your deductible to $1,000 or $2,500, which can reduce your premiums by as much as 30 percent. Then you'll avoid the temptation to submit small claims but still have the coverage for the big claims, which is really the reason to have homeowners' insurance. And you'll be more likely to qualify for a claims-free discount, which could reduce your premiums by 25 percent to 35 percent after seven to ten years without a claim.

The best step for you to take right now is to add up how much money you think you'd get from the insurer, subtract your deductible, and then decide whether or not it's still worthwhile to submit the claim.

I'm about to buy a new house and I need to get homeowners' insurance. How do I figure out how much homeowners' insurance to get?

That's the trickiest part of buying homeowners' insurance, and the reason why many people end up buying too much or too little coverage.

Your home's insurance value is very different from its market value. The price of the home includes the house as well as the land; the insurance value is only the cost to rebuild the house. If a fire burns down your home entirely, you'll still have the land.

A contractor in your area can give you a general estimate of local construction costs per square foot, which you could multiply by the total area of your home. But the real replacement cost will vary depending on the quality of the materials in your house and any special architectural features. It's best to have an appraiser or an agent come to your home and calculate the replacement cost. Or you can run the numbers yourself through a Web site such as AccuCoverage (*www.accucoverage.com*; cost, $7.95), which uses the estimates that builders use. It only takes about 10 to 15 minutes to type in details about your house—the square footage, age, materials, and special details—and you'll be given the same type of replacement cost that insurance companies use.

Also be sure to call your agent or insurance company if you make any major home improvements—especially if you add an addition to your home. Otherwise, those changes won't be covered. Insurance companies used to pay to replace your home no matter how much it cost; now, they generally cap your coverage at 125 percent of the insurance amount you've purchased—no matter how much it actually costs to rebuild your home. Your insurer may increase the coverage amount to keep up with general inflation numbers, but it may not be enough to keep up with rising building costs in your area, and it definitely won't be enough to cover extra additions.

Don't worry about the replacement estimate increasing your insurance cost by too much; you can often boost your coverage amount by $100,000 for as little as about $50 per year.

Are there any big expenses that generally aren't covered by homeowners' insurance?

The biggest gap is flood coverage, which isn't covered by homeowners' insurance policies and can cause serious damage even if you're far from the coast. In fact, 25 percent of all flood-loss claims are filed in low- to moderate-risk areas, according to the National Flood Insurance Program, the federal government's program that sells flood insurance. If you live in a low-risk area, you could get the maximum $250,000 coverage on your home and $100,000 on your possessions for less than $360 per year. There's usually a 30-day waiting period before the coverage takes effect.

The insurance is provided through the National Flood Insurance Program but sold by local agents. You can either contact your homeowners' insurance agent about the coverage or find a local agent through

FloodSmart.gov, where you can also get price quotes for the coverage.

That maximum $250,000 coverage from the federal program, however, may not be enough to rebuild your home. If your regular homeowners' insurance limits are higher than that, ask your insurer if it offers excess flood coverage that pays out after you max out the national flood program limits.

Many people with hurricane damage are also surprised by the limited coverage for fallen trees, and the out-of-pocket costs with which they end up. Insurers will generally cover damage to your house caused by fallen trees and about $500 for removal, but they generally provide no coverage if the tree doesn't hit your home.

If you are in a hurricane-prone area, you may be surprised by the size of your deductible. Many Floridians have percentage-based deductibles on their windstorm coverage—generally 2 percent to 5 percent of their home's coverage. That's $6,000 to $15,000 on a $300,000 home that they'd have to pay themselves before their homeowners' insurance kicked in. If that's the case for you, it's generally a good idea to make sure you have enough money in your emergency fund before hurricane season to cover your deductible and other potentially big out-of-pocket costs, such as tree removal.

I'm shopping around for homeowners' insurance and want to find a company that won't fight with me about claims; I've had some bad experiences in that area in the past. Is there any way that I can find out more about the customer service records for the companies I'm considering?

That's a great idea. Customer service makes a huge difference in homeowners' insurance. As we all saw after Hurricane Katrina, two homes can have similar damage from the same storm, but one homeowner can get his claim check quickly and start making repairs, while his next-door neighbor's home lingers with a blue tarp over the roof because the homeowner continues to fight with the insurance company to get his money. The experience can be totally different depending on the company you select.

State insurance regulators keep track of customer complaints, and most make it easy to check out a company's record at the insurance department's Web site. For links to your state's regulator, visit *www.naic.org*.

The most important piece of information is the insurer's complaint ratio—the number of complaints made for every dollar collected in premiums. With that figure, large insurers aren't unfairly penalized for more complaints just because they do more business. See how the insurance company's ratio compares to other insurers in your state. Also see if the insurance department has taken any actions against the company, such as levying fines for slow payment or claims-handling problems.

It also helps to check out the insurer's complaint record on a national database. Go to the National Association of Insurance Commissioners' Consumer Information Source (*www.naic.org/cis*), type in the company name, and select your state and "Property/Casualty" for the business type (that narrows the list to homeowners' and auto insurance). Click on "Closed Complaints" and then "Complaint Ratio Report," and select "Homeowners" as the insurance type. Click "Create Report" to get the full report details.

You'll see the insurer's complaint ratio, as well as a graph illustrating how that number compares to the national average. If the insurer's complaint ratio is worse than average, you may want to search for another company—even if the premiums are a little higher. Paying a few extra dollars for a company with a better track record can make a huge difference if you ever have a claim.

Because of these records, it's also important to notify the state insurance department if you have a complaint with your insurer. Not only can the regulator step in and help get your claim paid, but you'll go on record to show other customers about the company's problems.

My son is about to start his freshman year in college. Will my homeowners' insurance cover all the things he's planning to bring to his dorm room?

Your son's stuff is probably safe. Children are generally covered by their parents' homeowners' insurance if they're living in a dorm. But ask your agent or company about any limitations. Some policies, for example, limit protection to 10 percent of your total coverage for possessions.

Your homeowners' policy generally won't cover a child who lives in an off-campus apartment. In that case, buy a renters' policy, which tends to cost $200 to $300 per year and will cover his stuff as well as liability if anyone is injured in his apartment. Be sure to tell the insurer whether your child's name is on the lease.

While you're talking with your insurer, also ask about auto insurance discounts. If your son moves 100 miles or more from home for college and leaves the family car at home, your auto insurance premium may drop by up to 30 percent, yet he'll still be covered when he's home on vacation.

Life Insurance

I'm a 35-year-old single federal employee with 15 years of service. I have two kids and own one house. How much life insurance do I need and what type of insurance should I be looking for?

With two kids depending on you, you should definitely have life insurance. A basic rule of thumb is to buy eight to ten times your income. Because you're a single parent, you'll probably need a bit more. To get a more specific figure, check out the life insurance needs calculator at Kiplinger.com, which will help you add up your family's expenses, subtract income they'll have after you die, and figure out how much insurance you need to fill in that gap. Stay-at-home parents should run their numbers through an insurance-needs calculator, too, because their families will need to pay for child care and other expenses if they die, even though they aren't earning an income now.

You probably have life insurance through your job, but it's also good to get coverage that doesn't depend on your employment. And the price is probably much less than you'd expect. A healthy 35-year-old woman would only pay less than $400 per year for a $500,000 term insurance policy with a guarantee that rates won't rise for 20 years. She'd pay about $450 per year for a policy with a 30-year rate guarantee.

The length of term you should get depends on the age of your children and length of your mortgage. If your kids are young and you have a 30-year mortgage, you might want to pay extra for the 30-year term policy, which should last you until retirement and doesn't cost that much extra. If your kids are older and your mortgage is shorter, then 20 years may be enough. Even if you decide that you need the insurance for only ten years or so, it doesn't hurt to get at least a 20-year policy; you'll only pay about $100 extra per year to lock in an extra decade of coverage.

It's quick and easy to get price quotes from several companies at Web sites such as AccuQuote.com, Insure .com, and InsWeb.com. If you have any medical conditions, it's better to call the agents at the site—or an agent in your area—rather than just submitting your information online. That way, they can immediately lead you toward companies that are likely to offer the best rate for people with your type of health history.

An insurance agent gave me a quote for a term insurance policy, but after I actually applied, the price ended up being a few hundred dollars more. He said that I couldn't qualify for that company's best rate because of my cholesterol level. Should I go with the rate they've given me or should I shop around some more?

You should definitely shop around some more. Insurance companies are making it much more difficult to qualify for their best rates, and their second-best rates often cost hundreds of dollars more per year. But each company has different criteria to get its lowest prices, so you may qualify for the best rate with another insurer, which could cost you much less than the first company's second-best rate.

A 30-year-old male shopping on insurance marketplace InsWeb.com, for example, could pay as little as $275 per year for a $500,000 policy with a 20-year rate guarantee if his cholesterol HDL ratio is under 5.0. But if his HDL ratio is 5.0—not below it—the lowest rate he can get at InsWeb.com is $285, which is offered by another company. If his HDL is 5.1, the lowest rate he could get would be $330, which is offered by a third company. If he only applied with that first company and his HDL ended up being 5.0 or above, however, he'd get stuck paying at least $345—that insurer's second-best rate.

This is also why it's important to know all of your information when you get price quotes, including your cholesterol level, HDL, blood pressure, accurate height and weight, and family medical history. The insurer will double check this information when conducting a medical exam, but you're more likely to get an accurate price if you have a good idea of what they'll find and share that information up front. Online insurance brokerage Insure.com even shows the company's underwriting criteria with its quotes, explaining exactly what you need to do to qualify for the rate being quoted.

I was just shopping for life insurance and the agent asked me about my driving record. Could this really affect my rate? It seems like it wouldn't have much to do with life insurance.

Many life insurance companies have been using driving records as one of their pricing criteria for a while, charging you more if you've had several moving violations in the past few years. When you think about it, there is a correlation; people with bad driving records are more likely to get into accidents, which is one cause of early death.

But what is surprising is how strict the companies have become. You used to be able to get a company's lowest rate as long as you had no more than three moving violations in the past two years (assuming you also qualify healthwise). Now some companies knock you out of that preferred rate if you have two moving violations in three years.

This is just part of a trend by insurers to make it tougher to qualify for their lowest rates. They're also looking more carefully at your cholesterol HDL level, your blood pressure and any medication you are taking to control your blood pressure, your family medical history (including if any relative had certain diseases, whether or not they died from them), and your height and weight. Even though many term insurance companies have lowered their rates over the past few years, it's becoming much more difficult to get those best rates.

But the good news is that each company has different pricing criteria, so one that won't give you the lowest rate if your cholesterol is less than perfect may not penalize you if you have a few speeding tickets. Another might focus more on your family's medical history, but allow you to weigh more for your height than other insurers.

Because each company has different standards, it's essential to shop around before buying term life insurance, especially at a Web site or through an agent who works with many companies and asks a lot of medical questions before quoting you a price.

My employer is giving workers the chance to buy extra life insurance at group rates during open enrollment season this fall. Is that usually a good deal?

If you're in good health, you can probably find a less-expensive policy elsewhere. If you're in bad health, however, this might be your best option.

Many employers provide some life insurance coverage as a free benefit for employees. That's a great deal, but it's usually only about the same amount as your annual income, which is much less insurance than most people need. It's a good idea to supplement that coverage with additional life insurance that you can keep after you leave the job.

But the coverage that many employers offer beyond that employee benefit generally costs healthy people more than they'd pay if they bought a policy on their own. That's because many of these "voluntary enrollment" group policies ask few or no questions about your health. As a result, they assume that a certain number of unhealthy people will sign up, which boosts prices for everyone.

If you buy life insurance on your own, on the other hand, the insurer will ask a lot of questions about your medical condition, family history, risky hobbies, and travel, and will generally require you to take a quick medical exam. If you're in good health, you may pay as much as 50 percent less for an individual policy than you would for coverage under a group plan.

I recently started a job that doesn't include group life insurance, and I'd like to buy my own policy to provide coverage at least until my kids go to college. But I'm worried that I might not qualify for insurance because I'm a breast cancer survivor. My treatment ended three years ago and I've been cancer-free since then, but I'm still concerned that it might make it impossible to get life insurance. What should I do?

Start shopping around now and get help from an insurance broker who works with several companies. They'll usually know from experience which ones are more likely to accept someone with your medical condition and how to present the strongest case.

You might be very surprised by the results. A few years ago, most insurers would reject people who had breast cancer or require them to wait a few years before covering them, then charge very high rates. But because of medical advances, a handful of insurance companies now make it much easier for people with certain medical conditions—such as breast cancer, prostate cancer, and well-controlled diabetes—to get coverage.

For example, Hartford Life Insurance Company now offers policies at standard rates for women age 40 and older that have had breast cancer, as long as the patient had a small, localized Stage 1 condition and has a strong prognosis for survival. Candidates must also have completed treatment and the first follow-up visit with no evidence of the disease. But they don't need to wait years before getting coverage, as they'd need to do in the past. Several other insurers now have similar rules for breast cancer survivors.

And some insurers are now making it easier for people who had prostate cancer to get coverage soon after their treatment. Hartford offers standard rates, for example, to prostate cancer survivors who are age 60 or older and have been surgically treated (biopsy or radiation alone doesn't qualify), have a Gleason score of 6 or less, have a pretreatment PSA of 10 or less, and have the cancer confined to the prostate.

People with diabetes may be able to get coverage from some companies if they have good test results and can show that they're controlling the disease.

The rules can vary a lot from company to company, and the way you present the case can make a difference. Byron Udell, CEO of AccuQuote, a brokerage that works with dozens of insurance companies, generally puts together a package for the insurer that emphasizes the applicant's strengths, beyond just the information on the application, such as a letter that details how well the person is controlling the condition and highlights key information from the person's doctor.

It's essential to tell brokers or insurers up front about the condition; they'll find out through your medical records, anyway, so it's better to tell them at the beginning so they can only focus on insurers they know tend to offer the best deals for someone with your health history. And if you get rejected by one insurer, keep trying. Each one has very different rules for certain medical conditions, and one company may reject you entirely while another offers a decent rate.

Both my wife and I have existing term life insurance policies for $200,000 each. These policies have eight years left on them. We will be 56 and 54 years old when they expire. At that time, our two teenage boys should be out on their own. Would you recommend continuance of this term policy at the applicable rates for our age at the time of renewal or do you have any other suggestions?

The rate can jump significantly if you keep your old policy after the term is up, so it's generally better to shop around for a new one if you're still healthy. But instead of waiting until the policy term is up in eight years, see if you can get a better deal now. Term life insurance rates have dropped at an extraordinary pace over the past decade. In 1994, a healthy 40-year-old man would have to pay at least $995 for a $500,000 term life insurance policy with a 20-year rate guarantee. That same policy costs as little as $365 now.

After about ten years of consistently falling, term life insurance rates have generally stabilized. If you're healthy, you can still find a much better rate—or lock in the same rate for a longer time period—even if you bought a policy just a few years ago. Who knows what will happen to insurance rates—or your health—over the next eight years? If you think you might need coverage beyond that time period, it's a good idea to shop around for a longer-lasting policy now.

You can quickly get price quotes for many life insurance companies at Web sites such as AccuQuote.com, Insure.com, and InsWeb.com. A healthy 48-year-old man can buy a $200,000 policy with a 15-year rate guarantee for less than $370 per year; or pay less than $450 per year for a 20-year guarantee. When deciding how long a rate guarantee to get, consider how long you might be supporting your children or spouse, paying a mortgage, or anything else that is depending on your income. Because rates are so low, it doesn't hurt to buy a rate guarantee for a bit longer so you won't have to worry about shopping around later if you end up needing insurance for longer than expected. For help calculating how much life insurance to buy, check out the life insurance needs calculator at Kiplinger.com.

A couple of years ago, my wife and I were looking for a good way to supplement our main retirement savings, start a college fund, and get life insurance. When we started looking for ways to achieve these financial goals, we were steered in the direction of variable life insurance policies. I am 28 years old and my wife is 27. We are both healthy and in good shape. We do not have children yet but we plan on having them in the near future, and we haven't been maxing out our 401(k)s or Roth IRAs. We pay $155 a month ($1,860 per year) for my $300,000 policy and $80 a month for my wife's $200,000 policy, which we bought last year. Are we paying too much for these policies? Is there a better way to invest our money to accomplish our goals?

You're paying way too much for those policies, and there are much better ways to reach your goals. You could buy a 20-year term insurance policy with the same $300,000 death benefit for as little as $173 per year. Right now you're paying more than ten times that much every year for exactly the same amount of insurance. You could even buy a 30-year term policy for just $260 per year.

The variable life insurance policy does provide an investment account as well as life insurance, but you pay a slew of extra fees before any money is invested, including insurance costs that are sometimes double or triple the price of a term policy, plus front-end loads of up to 5 percent of each premium, and administrative charges as much as $10 per month ($120 per year).

You have much better ways to save without those extra fees. First, you should max out your 401(k)s, which lower your taxable income, grow tax deferred, and can earn you free money from an employer match. You and your wife can also contribute up to $4,000 per year to each of your Roth IRAs, which you can access tax free in retirement and withdraw the contributions without a penalty at any time. And you can invest in a 529 plan for tax-free college savings. You could even open up a 529 in your own name now and then transfer the beneficiary to your children after they're born.

Plus, long-term capital gains tax rates have dropped so low—15 percent or less—that you could even come out ahead by buying and holding stocks or funds in a taxable account.

If your agent didn't mention these options, it sounds like he was just trying to earn a big commission. Cash-value life insurance policies can work for some people who need insurance for more than 30 years, if they're worried about a big estate-tax bill, own a business, or have special-needs children, for example. But it's not the best choice for young couples who have many other less-expensive options and may not even need life insurance yet.

Auto Insurance

What's the easiest way to lower my auto insurance rates?

Auto insurance rates vary enormously from company to company for the exact same car and person, just based on the insurer's own experience. So the easiest way to lower your auto insurance rate is to shop around and see what other companies are offering. You may be able to cut your premiums by hundreds of dollars just by switching companies.

Now is a particularly good time to shop around for auto insurance because many major companies are in the midst of changing their pricing structure. In the past, they looked at a handful of variables when setting prices, such as your car, driving record, your age, and where you live. But because of advanced computing capabilities, they can now look at those and other features in a lot more detail when assessing the risk that you'll have a claim. For example, instead of just looking at damage and theft claim payments for the car you're considering, which has been a key factor in determining collision and comprehensive premiums for many years, they're also looking at the cost of injury claims to passengers in that type of car, and more recently, they started looking at claim payment amounts for damages that car does to other vehicles and their occupants, which affects the cost of your liability coverage. They're also looking more closely at how many miles you drive, and they now study dozens of data points within your credit report.

Because of these changes, people with good driving and credit records and safe cars may be able to lower their auto insurance prices by up to 25 percent. And people who had bad driving records may finally be able to get coverage from a regular company, instead of being rejected and shunned to a high-risk insurer.

It's easy to shop around. Check out price-quote Web sites such as InsWeb.com and Insure.com, which provide prices for several companies. Also visit a few insurers' Web sites, such as Progressive.com, StateFarm.com, and Allstate.com. You also can get help from an independent insurance agent who works with many companies (go to *www.iiaba.org* to find an agent in your area). Some state insurance departments also publish rate comparisons; find links to your state site at *www.naic.org*.

Because of these changes, buying a safe car can also make a big difference in your auto insurance rate. You can look up the car's cost to insure at StateFarm.com. There you can find the car's relative insurance costs in three categories: the damage and theft index grade (how its collision and comprehensive premiums stack up against vehicles in its price range), the liability rating index score (how premiums for bodily injury and property damage liability compare), and the car's vehicle safety discount, which is the discount for medical payments or personal injury protection coverage, based on the cost of claims involving injury to the occupants of the insured car. These ratings are from State Farm's claims experience and may be different for other companies. You can also look up a car's crash test results at the Insurance Institute for Highway Safety Web site (*www.carsafety.org*).

Another easy way to lower your premiums is to raise your deductibles and drop redundant coverage. Increasing your deductibles from $250 to $1,000 can lower your premiums by 15 percent or more and make you less likely to file small claims that could cost you a claims-free discount. You can also save some money by lowering your medical payments coverage. This coverage can be helpful to provide basic medical payments in case someone is injured in your car, regardless of who is at fault. But it generally duplicates your family's and your passengers' health insurance coverage. Get enough medical payments coverage to cover your health insurance deductible, but you generally don't need much more than $1,000 to $5,000.

And make sure you're getting all of the discounts you deserve. Most insurers will reduce your rates if you have your homeowners' and auto insurance with the same company, if the young drivers in your family maintain at least a B average in school, if your car has special safety and antitheft devices, and if you don't commute with the car and keep the annual mileage low. You may also get up to a 20 percent discount if nobody on the policy has had an at-fault accident or moving violation within the past three or five years. The specific discounts vary by company and state, so ask each insurer you're considering about the rate reductions you could get.

Why do auto insurance companies use credit scores when setting rates? What does that have to do with my driving record?

Surprisingly, your credit history has a lot to do with your driving record. When studying their claims records, insurers found that people with poor credit scores tend to have more claims than people with higher scores.

The Texas Department of Insurance conducted its own study in 2004 to see if there really was a correlation and came to the same conclusion. After studying the claims records of two million insurance policies, the insurance department found "the difference in claims experience by credit score was substantial," according to the regulator's report. The 10 percent of policyholders with the worst credit scores had 1.5 to 2 times more claims than the 10 percent of policyholders with the best credit scores. Drivers with the best credit scores were involved in about 40 percent fewer accidents than those with the worst credit scores.

A few states limit insurers' use of credit scores when setting premiums or deciding whom to insure, because they're concerned that the practice could discriminate against low-income people and minorities. And a few insurers don't use credit scores in their pricing. But most of them do, and each has its own variation on the calculation to determine your insurance score, based on its own claims history. Regardless of the insurer's specific formula, improving your credit record and credit score will also improve your insurance score. See Chapter 4, Credit and Debt, for advice on improving your credit score.

My son just started driving and our auto insurance premiums went up by almost $2,000 per year! Is there anything I can do to make that a little less painful?

It is always scary to get that first auto insurance bill after your teenager starts driving. Adding a teenage daughter to your policy typically boosts your price by 50 percent; adding a teenage son can increase your premiums by 100 percent—or more—according to the Insurance Information Institute. And that's even before they get their first ticket or accident.

But taking a few key steps can often cut those premiums in half.

First, make sure you're getting credit for all of the discounts you deserve. If your child has a B average or better, most insurers offer a good-student discount, which can shave up to 30 percent off their premium. Some insurers offer a discount for teenagers who have completed drivers' education (although many don't because they found those classes had minimal value in terms of lowering their risk). A few insurers even offer their own educational programs for young drivers, which can reduce your rate by about 10 percent. The details and discount size vary a lot by company, state, and person. State Farm's Steer Clear Driver Discount gives a discount for all male and unmarried female drivers under age 25 who have had no at-fault accidents or moving violations in the past three years and have completed a special program administered by a State Farm agent that includes a video presentation, reading a safe-driving magazine, and completing a driver's log to document driving experiences.

Also make the most of your other discounts by insuring your home and auto with the same company and maintaining a spotless driving record yourself. Because your premiums are so high right now, it's a particularly important time for everyone in the family to avoid accidents and tickets, which can earn you a good driver discount of about 20 percent.

The car your child drives can also make a big difference in the price. It's generally cheapest to add your child to your policy as an occasional driver, rather than getting him his own policy. And pairing him with your safest car will help a lot too. Not just an old car, which might not have up-to-date safety features, but a safe car. You can get a list of the safest cars from the Insurance Institute for Highway Safety (*www.carsafety.org*). The 2006 Top Safety Pick awards include the Ford Five Hundred and Mercury Montego for large cars, the Subaru

Legacy and Saab 9-3 for midsize cars, and the Honda Civic for small cars.

To see the effect these types of cars can have on your insurance rates, check out the vehicle ratings at the State Farm Web site (*www.statefarm.com*) or the Make and Model Comparison Tool at Allstate's Web site (*www.allstate.com*).

Raising your deductibles to at least $1,000 can help too. And if the car is worth less than a few hundred dollars, you can drop your comprehensive and collision coverage entirely. To check out your car's value, see the Kelley Blue Book Web site (*www.kbb.com*).

It also doesn't hurt to compare prices from other companies; some insurers don't really want to insure teenage drivers and jack up the cost a lot more than others. You can check out prices at InsWeb.com, State-Farm.com, Allstate.com, Progressive.com, or by contacting an independent agent (find one in your area at *www.iiaba.org*). If a family member is in the military, also check out the United Services Automobile Association (USAA) at *www.usaa.com.*

If I total my car, will my insurance company pay the amount I owe the bank on my car loan?

Maybe not. Most auto insurance policies will only pay you for the car's current market value as a used car, which is usually much less than what you originally paid when it was new. Even cars that are just a few weeks old generally depreciate significantly the minute you drive them off the lot.

If you took out a four- or five-year loan, the insurance payout may not be enough to pay off your loan—even if you've already been making payments for several months. It's becoming more common for people to be upside-down on their car loans, which means they owe more than their car is worth, because they're taking out longer loans while many cars are depreciating faster than they had in the past (often because car companies are offering big rebates or sales on new models, which forces the prices down on used cars).

To estimate whether you could have this problem, go to Kelley Blue Book's Web site (*www.kbb.com*) and look up how much one-year-old models of the car you're considering are worth. This isn't the exact number the insurance company will use, but it can give you a general idea of how much you could get. Then compare that amount to what you still owe on your loan. Use the "How Much Will My Vehicle Payments Be?" calculator at Kiplinger.com to see the balance at various points in a loan's life.

If you do owe more than your insurer will pay, you can solve the problem by buying gap insurance, which lenders and insurance companies offer to cover the difference between a car's cash value when it's totaled and the amount you still owe the lender. The price is usually minor, averaging about $45 per year from Progressive, for example, or up to $500 or $600 for the life of the loan from many lenders and dealers. (You may be able to negotiate a lower price from dealers in many states.) Some companies, such as MetLife, include some additional coverage in their standard auto insurance policies at no extra cost—they'll automatically pay the full cost to buy a new car if you total your car within the first year and have driven less than 15,000 miles.

Gap insurance is worth the cost only if you face a potential gap of several thousand dollars. You generally don't need it if you make a down payment of 20 percent or more. Keep in mind that you may need the coverage for just a year or two, because as time passes, the size of the gap shrinks.

I'm going to be out of the country for a few months for business and I am putting my car in storage. Should I drop my auto insurance while I'm gone?

Don't drop the coverage while your car is in storage. Insurers like to see that you've had continuous coverage; otherwise, they worry that you've been driving without insurance, which can make it tough to find an affordable policy when you return if you haven't had insurance for a while—as several soldiers unfortunately discovered when they returned from Iraq. Depending on your state laws, you may need to keep minimum liability limits unless you turn in your license plates, and it's best to keep some coverage anyway in case anything happens to your car while it's stored away.

There's an easy way to lower your premiums while keeping some insurance. Eliminate collision coverage entirely; if nobody is driving your car, then it's unlikely to be in an accident. Keep comprehensive coverage, which will protect your car if it's damaged or stolen while in storage; but because that's unlikely to happen, you can lower your premiums significantly by raising your deductible to $1,000 or even $2,500. Then lower your liability limits to your state's minimum (often about $25,000 per person/$50,000 per accident) and drop all extra coverage such as rental car, towing, and medical payments coverage. And tell your insurer that you'll be away and won't be driving the car, which can also give you a low-mileage discount. Making all of these changes could lower your premiums by as much as 75 percent, yet still give you some coverage if anything happens to your car while you're gone.

If you already dropped your coverage and do have problems resuming the insurance after you return, be sure to tell the insurance company the reason why you didn't have insurance. Fortunately, after complaints to regulators and a lot of bad publicity, the insurance companies eventually ended up reinstating coverage for the soldiers.

Long-Term Care Insurance

Is it worth it to buy long-term care insurance? And is there any way to lower the cost?

It's definitely worthwhile for most people to buy long-term care insurance. The average nursing home room currently costs about $75,000 per year, and round-the-clock care in your home can cost even more. If the price of care continues to rise by about 5 percent per year, the bill could top $250,000 per year by the time today's 55-year-old is likely to need care. And with nursing home stays averaging about 2.5 years, your total bill could add up to more than $600,000, which could quickly drain your retirement accounts, leaving you and your spouse with little savings and your heirs without an inheritance.

Instead of worrying about those astronomical bills, it's much easier to pay a few thousand dollars a year to buy long-term care insurance.

Long-term care policies with lifetime coverage and all the bells and whistles can cost a 55-year-old nearly $5,000 per year for a $200 daily benefit that increases by 5 percent every year. But you can easily lower the annual cost while still getting a good deal of coverage.

First, start by slashing the benefit period. A study by Milliman, an actuarial consulting firm, found that 92 percent of the 70-year-old claimants had claims of five years or fewer. Shortening the benefit period from lifetime to five years can reduce your annual premiums by about $2,000. Shrinking the benefit period down to three years can cut your costs even further. It may be worthwhile to pay extra for a longer benefit period, however, if you have a family history of Alzheimer's or other long-lasting conditions.

Then, extend the waiting period. A John Hancock policy with a $200 daily benefit, three-year benefit period, 5 percent inflation protection, and 30-day waiting period would cost a 55-year-old about $2,430 per year. Extending the waiting period to 90 days can lower the annual premiums to $2,025. But you don't want to increase your waiting period much longer than that; otherwise you'll have to pay huge bills from your own pocket before the coverage kicks in, which will be in tomorrow's dollars. If the cost of care increases by 5 percent per year, a 180-day waiting period in 25 years could result in a $122,000 bill before your policy pays out.

Finally, see if you can get a spousal discount or shared-care benefit. Spousal discounts can shave as much as 40 percent off your costs yet give each spouse the same amount of coverage. And several companies now offer shared-care benefits, which give you and your spouse a pool of benefits and cut the costs even more. With a six-year shared-care benefit, you'll get six years between the two of you; if one spouse needs care for two years, the other will still have four years of benefits available. A 55-year-old couple buying a six-year shared-care policy from John Hancock with a $200 daily benefit and a 90-day waiting period would pay about $4,400 per year for the combined coverage.

At what age should I consider buying long-term-care insurance?

In the past, people generally didn't start to think about buying long-term care insurance until age 65. But many people have started to buy the policies a lot earlier, as they discover how important the coverage can be to protect their retirement savings.

There's no advantage to waiting to buy coverage because the rates for a new policy increase every year with your age, plus new policies are priced about 20 percent to 40 percent higher than they were just a few years ago. No matter when you buy, you'll probably end up paying about the same amount over your lifetime.

For example, if you purchase insurance today at age 55 for a fixed premium of $900 a year and you don't need care until age 80, you'll have spent about $22,500 in premiums. A 65-year-old who buys a policy today with an annual premium of $1,500 and also doesn't need care until age 80 would pay the same amount, $22,500. Buying earlier means you forgo investing elsewhere, but you'd be buying an extra ten years of protection. There's always the slight possibility that you end up with a medical condition that requires long-term care well before retirement, or at least that you'd develop a health problem that makes it much more difficult, or expensive, to buy the coverage at all.

The bigger question is whether you can afford the coverage. Before buying long-term-care insurance, take care of more immediate financial needs—adequate life and disability insurance, an emergency fund, and retirement savings. When you no longer need life insurance to protect your family, that's a good time to drop that coverage and shift your premium payments to a long-term-care policy.

How do I figure out how much long-term care insurance to get?

S tart by checking out the cost of care in your area. The average daily cost of a private room in a nursing home is $203 across the country, according to the MetLife Mature Market Institute. But the actual numbers vary a lot from city to city. The average daily cost is $135 in Birmingham, Alabama, and $330 in San Francisco. And round-the-clock care in your home can cost even more. The average hourly rate for a home health aide varies just as much; it's $13 in Birmingham and $21 in San Francisco.

To figure out how much coverage you need, first check out prices for facilities you wouldn't mind utilizing in your area. Then figure out how much of the bill you could shoulder yourself and buy enough coverage to fill in the gap. The key is to think of the costs in future dollars—just like you would the rest of your retirement expenses.

My employer is letting me buy long-term care insurance as an employee benefit. Is that the best way to get coverage?

N ot necessarily. You'd think if you work for a big employer that it's getting a special deal when it lets you buy long-term care insurance at work, but you may find a much better deal on your own—especially if you're healthy and married. In fact, group policies tend to cost participants 20 percent to 40 percent more than individual policies for the same coverage.

One reason is because many group policies offer coverage to all employees regardless of their health (called "guaranteed issue"). This can be a great deal if you have medical problems, but the healthy people end up subsidizing the unhealthy people, which boosts the costs for everyone. Most individual policies, on the other hand, offer big discounts for people in good health.

Many group policies also don't offer spousal discounts, which can be as high as 40 percent with some individual policies. And they rarely offer special benefits, such as shared-care coverage, which gives you and your spouse a pool of coverage to share. Before buying coverage at work, compare rates for individual policies with the big players, such as John Hancock, MetLife, Genworth, and New York Life.

I've been offered a choice between two types of inflation protection for my group long-term care insurance policy: one that keeps premiums level for the life of the policy but automatically increases the coverage amount by 5 percent every year to keep up with the rising costs of care, and another one that offers guaranteed purchase options, which starts out a lot cheaper but the premiums increase through the years as I add additional coverage. Which is the best choice?

The 5 percent inflation protection might look a lot more expensive now, but it's actually the most cost-effective choice over the long run.

It's essential to have some kind of inflation adjustment to keep up with the increasing cost of care. A policy with a $200 daily benefit will barely make a dent in the bills if care costs $677 per day when you eventually need it, leaving you with only $73,000 to cover an annual bill of nearly $250,000.

But there are several types of inflation protection, and some are a lot better than others.

The best coverage automatically increases the benefit amount by 5 percent compounded every year, which has been keeping pace with the rising cost of care. The coverage is pricey, often doubling the cost of the policy, but the premiums remain the same even though the benefit amount increases.

And you're right, there is another type of inflation protection that looks a lot cheaper at first, but it ends up being much more expensive over the long run. Policies with future purchase options don't automatically increase your benefit amount and can start out costing half as much as the policies with the 5 percent compound inflation do, but they let you buy additional coverage through time without any medical questions.

The problem is that the increases are generally priced at the age when you buy the extra coverage, not the age when you first bought the policy. And because the price of long-term care rises as you get older, these policies can become extraordinarily expensive at exactly the time when it's toughest to afford the premiums.

A study by Legacy Services Inc., an independent insurance agency specializing in long-term care insurance for large employers, illustrates the problem. If a 47-year-old buys a policy that starts with a $150 daily benefit, three-year benefit period, and 90-day waiting period, he'd pay $827 per year for automatic 5 percent compound inflation protection, or just $347 per year for a policy with future purchase options.

If he increases the benefit amount by 5 percent per year, the policy with the future purchase options (FPO) will get much more expensive each year while the compound inflation protection policy will remain the same—$1,158 per year for the FPO versus a stable $827 for the automatic 5 percent increases—even though both provide the same $364 in daily benefits.

The difference is even larger as he gets older. By age 80, when he's more likely to need care, the FPO policy will cost $7,811 per year while the other policy continues to cost $827, with both policies providing $756 in daily benefits.

You can always choose not to exercise some of the future purchase options, but then you could fall far short of the cost of care and have to make up the difference from your savings, which can be particularly difficult if you'd been counting on the policy to protect your retirement funds and you don't have the extra money to make up for the shortfall.

Disability Insurance

I have disability insurance through work. Do I need an individual policy too?

You may. Group disability policies through work do provide some helpful coverage, which protects part of your income if you become sick or injured and can't do your job. But they can leave some giant gaps. Most employer policies, for example, only cover 60 percent of your income, and the payouts will be taxable if your employer pays the premiums, which shrink your benefits even further.

The coverage limits are generally calculated from your base salary only, not commissions and bonuses, which can leave you with a lot less money than you're used to if you're in sales, on Wall Street, or in another profession where a big part of your income is paid that way.

Look at your policy or contact your company's human resources director and find out exactly how much income your group policy can provide you with each month. If that isn't enough to cover your expenses, then it is worthwhile to look into buying an individual policy.

Credit and Debt

Carrying too much debt can ruin the rest of your financial plans. If you're spending a lot of money in interest payments every month, you'll have so much less money to devote to your financial goals. But you can't avoid debt entirely, and it isn't even a good idea to try. Some debt, such as a mortgage and student loans, can provide a low-interest source of money to help you afford a valuable investment. But high interest credit card debt gets you nothing in return and just eats up your cash every month. Minimizing this type of debt—and understanding the harsh rules—can do wonders for your financial situation. But this is where it's great to hear from readers. Most people know how important it is to get rid of too much debt, but have trouble finding the cash to do so. Fortunately, there are many great strategies that can help you lower your interest rates, get help if you need it, and free up a lot of money.

And even if you feel like you're managing debt well, there are still several steps you can take to lower your interest rates even further and minimize other fees. One of the topics I get asked about the most is how to improve your credit score, and for good reason. This mysterious number, based on information from your credit report, has a huge impact on the rate you'll get on every type of loan. Improving your score by a few points can save you thousands of dollars in interest payments, whether you have a good or bad credit history. But people tend to make big mistakes when trying to raise their score.

Readers also ask a lot about which debt to pay off first, which makes a big difference in your financial situation too. Sometimes it pays to forego other goals for a while until you pay off your debt; other times it does not. There are actually solid answers to this question and a step-by-step solution, and some of the advice may surprise you. Here's what you need to know to manage your debt.

Improving Your Credit Score

I know that my credit score affects my mortgage rate. But do I need to worry about my score when I'm not about to buy a house?

You sure do. Your credit score, the numerical summary of how much you owe and how promptly you pay your bills, makes a big difference in your mortgage rate. But it also affects other less-obvious areas of your personal finances.

A good score can also save you thousands of dollars on your car loan and credit card interest payments. But a low score can make it tough to get a loan, and also to buy a cell phone, rent an apartment, or get a job. It may reduce the size of the mortgage you qualify for, or require that you make a bigger security deposit when you open an account with a phone service or electric utility. And it can make a surprisingly big difference in your auto insurance rate, because insurers discovered that people with low credit scores are much more likely to have claims than those with high scores.

What is a good credit score, and how can I improve my score?

FICO scores, the credit scores developed by Fair Isaac that most lenders use, range from 300 to 850, but only 13 percent of consumers have scores above 800. The median score is 723, and many lenders require a score of 760 or higher to get the best interest rates.

The scores are based on information from your credit reports, so the easiest way to improve your score is to make sure your report doesn't contain any errors. Go to AnnualCreditReport.com to order a free copy of your reports every 12 months from each of the three credit bureaus: Experian, Equifax, and TransUnion. It's essential to check all three reports for errors because some lenders get your scores from only one or two of the bureaus, while others may get all three and average the score. If you do find any mistakes, it's usually fastest to fix them online.

The best way to maintain a good score is to pay your bills on time. More than one-third of your score is based on your payment history, and the later you are, the more points you lose. If you've fallen behind, get caught up now. Negative items generally affect your score for up to seven years, but as time goes by their impact lessens.

How much you owe makes up another third of your score. Your "credit utilization" ratio—the percentage of your credit limit that you've actually used—is more important than the amount of credit to which you have access. It's generally best to keep the balance on your cards below 25 percent of your available credit, or $2,500 on a card with a $10,000 ceiling. What counts is the total amount you've charged when your score is checked, even if you plan to pay the bill in full.

The length of your credit history accounts for 15 percent of your FICO score. Getting a lot of new credit within a short time span can hurt your score because it lowers the average age of your accounts.

About 10 percent of your score is based on new credit. If you open a flurry of new accounts, lenders worry that you might go on a borrowing binge. It's best to avoid applying for new credit within three to six months of applying for a mortgage. Your credit report records an inquiry every time a potential lender requests a copy of the report, and that can make lenders nervous. Because more people shop online for car loans and mortgages, Fair Isaac eased its rules: If your report shows inquiries from several car or mortgage lenders within 14 days, it's assumed you're shopping for a single loan. The newest version of the FICO score expands that to 45 days.

Finally, 10 percent of your score depends on the types of credit you use. Your experience with revolving credit, such as credit cards, on which you control how much you charge and pay off each month, carries more weight than installment debt, such as car loans and mortgages, with fixed payments.

Are there things I can do that accidentally hurt my score?

There are a lot of misconceptions about what you can do to help or hurt your score. The biggest mistake people make is to close old accounts. You may think that getting rid of accounts you haven't used in a while can make your credit score look better. But closing old accounts can actually hurt your score because it raises your utilization ratio. Owing $5,000 looks a lot better when you have a $20,000 maximum on all of your credit cards—a utilization ratio of 25 percent—than it does after you close some cards and only have a total limit of $7,000. In that case, your ratio rises to more than 70 percent, which will hurt your score.

Even though your credit score will dip temporarily, it's okay to close accounts as long as you don't plan to apply for a loan within the next few months. That will give your score time to recover. But avoid closing old accounts that show you have a good credit history; having those accounts on your record improves your score. Close department-store accounts and new cards first.

Also, people have no idea how devastating some small items can be on your score—such as library fines or parking tickets—if they go to collection. The problem is becoming more common as local governments try to beef up their revenues and hire collection agencies to track down the money people owe in library fines, unpaid parking tickets, and other fees. If an account goes into collection, it can destroy your credit score, dropping a high FICO score by as much as 100 points.

A new version of the FICO score ignores delinquencies on accounts for which the past-due amount is less than $100. But most lenders still use the older version of the score. If you're disputing a small charge, it might be better to pay the bill rather than continue to fight or take the issue to small-claims court. Ask to have the collection accounts removed from your record in exchange for payment.

I was told that requesting my credit report and credit score is considered to be a hit on my credit score every time I do that. Is this true?

No. Your requests for your own credit information won't affect your score. In fact, it's a good idea to check your credit score and reports at least once per year to make sure there aren't any errors. You can order a free copy of your report from each of the three credit bureaus every 12 months at AnnualCreditReport.com.

Your credit report may include a long list of credit inquiries, recording whenever you, your current lenders, potential lenders, prospective employers, or others ask to see your report. But the FICO credit score only counts inquiries that were made when you applied for a loan. That way, potential lenders will have a heads up if it looks like you're applying for a lot of credit at once and may have a tough time paying your bills.

The FICO score has changed its rules about inquiries a bit over the past few years. As more people started to shop around for mortgage and car loan rates online, the scorekeepers realized that someone might be applying to multiple lenders at once just to compare rates but only planned to take out one loan.

As a result, the FICO score ignores all mortgage and auto inquiries made in the past 30 days. And if the FICO score finds clusters of inquiries made more than 30 days ago, it counts all of the inquiries made within that one shopping period as just one inquiry. For the older version of the FICO score, this shopping period is any 14-day span. The newer version of the FICO score, which many mortgage lenders don't use yet, expands the shopping period to any 45-day span.

I understand that when my credit score is calculated, one factor that's considered is my balance as a percentage of my credit limit. But my credit card issuer, Capital One, does not report credit limits to the credit bureaus, so a limit of $0 shows on my report. Can I do something to get around this policy and improve my score?

All Capital One customers should be as informed as you about the company's policy. Capital One doesn't report its customers' credit limits because the company considers it to be a proprietary part of their business.

But that policy can hurt your credit score. You're correct that when Fair Isaac compiles its so-called FICO scores, the company factors in what percentage of your credit limit you've actually used; the lower your utilization ratio, the better. In the absence of a credit limit, the FICO system substitutes the highest reported balance from that creditor.

Unfortunately, that means good payment habits on your account could accidentally result in a lower score. Let's say your credit limit is $10,000, but you've never owed more than $1,000 and you typically pay your bill in full each month. Then you charge $500. It looks like you're using 50 percent of your total credit available, even though your actual limit is much higher. It's usually best to keep your utilization ratio to 25 percent or less when you're about to apply for a loan.

If you're planning to borrow money for a house or a car, one way to keep your credit score high is to make a big purchase on your Capital One card at least six months before you plan to take out the loan. That would boost your highest balance and improve your utilization ratio, provided you paid the bill in full before any interest was due, and long before you take out a big loan.

Here's an even easier solution if you're about to take out a big loan: use the card of a different issuer, almost all of which do report credit limits. Capital One is a major player, but most credit card companies do report their customers' credit limits. To check on whether your issuer reports credit limits (and whether they're accurate), get a free copy of your credit report at *www.annualcreditreport.com* or by calling 877-322-8228.

My credit card company just increased the spending limit on my card. Will this help or hurt my credit score?

Increasing the limit on your card may actually improve your credit score. If you don't borrow more money, the higher limit lowers your credit utilization ratio, which is the percentage of your available credit that you've used. Lenders like you to use only a small percentage of your available credit so you don't appear to be maxing out your cards. Charging $3,000 when you have a $10,000 limit, for example, looks a lot better than charging $3,000 when your limit is only $5,000. It's the opposite situation from closing out old cards.

What are some resources that can help me learn more about my credit score?

The best resource is Fair Isaac's consumer Web site, myFICO.com, which goes into detail about what your score includes and lists steps for improving your number. Also check out its table listing how a few points' difference in your score can affect your mortgage rate—taken from daily polls of lenders' rates. You can order your score there and use its score simulator, which shows how much your score can improve by making specific moves.

For ordering your credit report, see AnnualCredit Report.com. Avoid companies with look-alike names. The Federal Trade Commission has cracked down on several companies for setting up sites with similar names as a ploy to get people to sign up for expensive credit-monitoring services. You won't be able to order your score free—just your credit report—but you may be able to get your score for as little as $7.95 when you're ordering your free report. It's most important to check your FICO score, not the proprietary scores some credit bureaus use, because that's the score most lenders use.

I am getting married in October. I have a lot of debt, but my fiancé has none. How can I prevent my bad credit from affecting him? Would separate accounts help?

Congratulations on your wedding and your concern for your new spouse. Usually, it's the spouse with good credit who's worried about having his or her record besmirched.

In your situation, maintaining separate accounts would certainly help. Each of you has your own credit report—there are no joint credit reports or scores—so your record shouldn't affect your husband's as long as you don't cosign for any credit. If you try to buy something jointly, however, both of your credit histories will be considered, and the worse report may have the bigger impact on the rate.

If you plan to buy a car or a house soon, see if you can get the loan in only your husband's name. Or wait until after you've improved your credit score to make a big purchase. Most negative items remain on your credit report for up to seven years, but they count for less as each year passes. You can usually turn your score around in two to three years. Take a look at the interest rates at myFICO.com to see how improving your score by a few points can make a huge difference in your mortgage rate.

Which Loans to Pay Off First

My husband and I have a lot of debt and we are spending about $1,000 monthly on credit card debt and about $3,100 on housing and car payments. We have just sold a rental home and netted about $30,000. My husband wants to invest it and watch it grow but I think we should try to get out of some of the debt we are in. What is your advice on how to use the sale proceeds?

Set your priorities based on interest rates, comparing the rate you're paying on the debt to your potential investment returns.

First, invest enough money in your 401(k) to get any employer match, which generally gives you 50 percent or 100 percent returns just from the match alone—a much higher rate than you're paying on the debt.

Then, use the rest of your money to pay down high-interest credit card debt. Balances on an 18 percent card are costing you a lot more than you could ever get from most investments. And add your car loan to the hierarchy based on its interest rate.

If you have a lot of high-interest debt, though, it's still a good idea to invest some of the money, too, so you don't get out of the saving habit entirely.

Next, use some cash to build up an emergency fund with three to six months of living expenses, so you don't land in debt again.

But there's some debt you don't need to worry about as much. Your student loans and mortgage, for example, are probably charging low rates and the interest may be tax deductible. It's usually better to invest the money rather than rushing to pay off either of those loans, especially if your investments can earn more than the interest they're charging.

My mortgage will be paid off by the end of the year. I am 45, my husband is 46, and we have a 9-year-old child and 4-year-old twins. Where should we be investing the money now that we will not be paying the mortgage anymore? We already max out our 401(k)s. Should we also maximize the children's 529 accounts, open an IRA or Roth IRA, invest in bonds, or should we use it to pay off our credit cards? Because we are used to paying the money every month, we want to find a good place to keep sending it now.

Congratulations on paying off your mortgage. What a huge accomplishment! You're very smart to start thinking about good uses for the money now, so you'll immediately be able to put it to good use before you even realize it's there. Because you've gotten used to paying out that money every month anyway, it's a great way to jump-start your savings or improve your financial situation without having to make any sacrifices.

Whenever you have a windfall, whether it's a raise, bonus, inheritance, or any extra cash—when you pay off your mortgage or car loan—there are usually a few moves that you should consider first: pay off any high-interest debt (such as credit card debt) and make sure you have three to six months' worth of living expenses in an emergency fund, so you don't need to sell investments or go into debt if you have any unexpected bills.

After that, make the most of your tax-advantaged savings options. That's great that you already contribute the maximum to your 401(k). You should contribute the maximum into a Roth IRA if you qualify (you need to earn less than $166,000 if married; $114,000 if single in 2007). That's $4,000 each in 2006, which translates into $333 per month for each of you to max out your Roth IRAs ($666 total).

Unless you had a tiny mortgage, you probably still have some money left over. It's also a perfect time to assess how well you're doing with your college savings. Run your numbers through a calculator like T. Rowe Price's college investment calculator to see if you're on track (available in the college planning section of *www. troweprice.com*). This calculator is great because it gives you the cost figures for specific schools and uses Monte Carlo simulations, which run your numbers through hundreds of potential investment scenarios to assess the likelihood that you'll have enough money to pay the bills.

If you need to boost your college savings, invest some of the extra money into 529s for the kids, which can be used tax free for college expenses, or into a Coverdell education savings account, if you qualify, where you can use the cash tax free for college as well as other educational expenses when your kids are in primary or secondary school.

How long will it take to pay off my credit card debt if I make the minimum monthly payment?

It takes a very, very long time to pay off your credit card debt if you only pay the minimum. Most card issuers set your minimum payment at 4 percent of your debt, so a $5,000 credit card balance with an 18 percent interest rate would start with a $200 monthly payment. But if you only make that minimum payment, it will take 12.5 years to pay off your credit card debt, during which time you'll pay the card company a total of $2,916 in interest—more than half the cost of the whole loan in interest payments. And that's assuming you don't make any new charges on the card! Credit card interest is wasted money that you could have used instead to help reach your financial goals.

The best advice is to ignore the card's minimum payment and pay as much as you can every month. Paying down a credit card with an 18 percent interest rate should be one of your very first financial priorities; the rate is probably a lot higher than any other loans you have and you're unlikely to find other investments to beat that rate (other than your employer's 401(k) match). Switching to a lower-rate card can make a big difference, too.

If you lower the rate to 6 percent and continue to make the minimum payment, it will take more than nine years to pay off the balance, and you'll pay a total of $696 in interest. But if you increase your monthly payments to $500, you'll pay off the balance in 11 months and pay a total of $142 in interest.

To run the numbers for your own situation, see "The True Cost of Paying the Minimum" calculator at Kiplinger.com.

I have a choice of financing a car with a 6 percent bank loan or putting it on a credit card with a 2.99 percent rate. Which would be the better deal on a $10,000 loan?

It may sound like a no-brainer, but be very careful about that 2.99 percent rate. A credit card rate is a lot different from a bank auto loan. Credit card companies can generally raise your rate with just 15 days' notice. They can also bump up the rate from 2.99 percent to, say 20 percent, if you're late with a single payment—on the low-rate card or any other outstanding debt. This "universal default" concept is becoming more common and is costing borrowers a lot of money.

In addition to the rate hike, you could also get hit with a late fee of $35 or more.

Read the disclosure agreement carefully to see exactly what could happen to the interest rate, and look for other loan options too. You can shop for auto-loan rates at Bankrate.com.

If the credit card deal checks out and you use it to buy the car, don't buy anything else with that card. Card companies generally charge higher interest rates for new purchases, and your payments go toward the lower-rate debt first. And resist the temptation to coast by making only the minimum payment. Figure out how much you'd need to send in each month to pay off the balance in no more than three or four years, just as if you had taken the bank loan.

Whether you shift this loan to the credit card or not, the new rules about late charges make it a good idea to sign up for online bill paying, where your monthly bills are paid automatically from your bank, so you'll be less likely to suffer expensive consequences if you miss your lender's deadline. And it's a good idea to check your credit report to make sure you aren't being penalized because of a mistake. You can order a free copy of your report from each of the three credit bureaus every 12 months from AnnualCreditReport.com.

A few of my credit cards charge higher rates than other cards I see advertised. What can I do to try to get the rate lowered? Do I need to switch cards? I'm always getting mailings from other cards with lower rates.

You may not need to switch to another card. Instead, use those low-rate mailings as leverage when you call your card company and ask for a lower rate. "Let them know that you've been using the card, or will start using the card, if they give you a better deal," says Scott Bilker, founder of DebtSmart.com and author of *Talk Your Way Out of Credit Card Debt*. "Read a few of the low-rate offers to the representative so they know you have options and that you will transfer your balances if they don't comply." If that person can't make the change, ask for the supervisor. "Be patient," says Bilker. "You may have to tell your story a few times."

It also doesn't hurt to ask the credit card company to waive the annual fees. "If the bank doesn't waive that, then remind them that there are many other cards that don't charge those fees and that you'll be using one of those banks shortly," he says.

If the credit card company won't waive the fee, Bilker's had luck asking the bank to change the card to a different product that doesn't charge a fee. "In other words, they were able to save face by refusing to remove the annual fee but not lose me by moving me to another card that didn't have the fee—with all other terms the same."

If the rate negotiation doesn't work, call your other credit card companies and ask if they have a low-rate transfer deal, says Bilker. Then transfer the high-rate balances to the low-rate card. However, you will need to keep track of any teaser rates; often the low transfer rate gets jacked up after six months or so. Perpetual switching can hurt your credit score, so it's best if you can pay the card off by the deadline.

Is it better to go with a low-interest credit card or a rebate card?

It all depends on how you use your card. If you don't carry a balance, you don't need to worry about the interest rate. Instead, focus on any annual fees and rebates. Several card companies offer good rebate programs with no annual fee. You can search for options at CardWeb.com (*www.cardweb.com*) or Bankrate.com (*www.bankrate.com*).

And if you do carry a balance, pay careful attention to the interest rate. A card may start by offering a low-interest teaser rate, but the rate could rise significantly after six months or so. You need to stay on top of these rate hikes and either pay off your balance or switch to another low-rate card before the teaser period is over, but be careful about any balance transfer fees.

Should I take a 0-percent credit card offer? What are the risks?

Take the credit card with the 0 percent teaser rate if you can pay off the balance before the rate expires, which is typically in 6 to 12 months. If you need longer, then look for a card with a low fixed rate.

And read the fine print. Some cards waive fees only on your first balance transfer. Additional transfers may have to pay a fee of up to 4 percent—that's $400 on a balance transfer of $10,000.

And you may need good credit to qualify; a 3.99 percent rate may rise to 5.99 percent if your credit score isn't quite as high.

Be careful of low-rate transfer offers on an existing card that already has a balance. Your payments will be used to pay down the lower-rate balance first, and interest will continue to accrue on the initial balance that has the higher rate.

I never got a credit card while I was in college. Now that I've graduated, what's the best way to get one?

Start with a secured card. You'll have to deposit between $100 and $500 in a savings account to acquire a line of credit equal to that amount (a few issuers offer credit limits that are double the deposit amount). You'll earn interest on your deposit, but you won't be able to withdraw your money until the account is closed.

Nearly every secured card charges an annual fee, but you should never pay a processing or application fee. Interest rates run from 10 percent to 30 percent, so shop carefully (go to *www.cardlocator.com*).

Make sure the issuer will report card activity to all credit agencies (so that you can build a credit history) and will let you upgrade to an unsecured card after a year of making regular on-time payments.

My wife got three credit cards in her name and proceeded to run up balances of about $5,000 on each one, at 12 percent interest. Then she lost her job. I have taken over the payments, which stretches our budget. What options do we have? If she defaults, what will be the consequences?

The most important advice is not to miss any payments. If she does, she'll get hit with late fees, her credit report will suffer, and her interest rate may rise, which will make it even tougher to pay off the debt.

You can avoid these problems by paying at least the minimum every month. But paying the minimum alone will kill you with interest costs. If you make the minimum payment every month (probably $200 on a $5,000 debt), it will take you more than ten years to pay off the credit card, and you'll pay more than $1,600 in interest over that time. And that's just for one card.

Boosting your monthly payments on each card to $500 can make a huge difference. In that case, it will only take 11 months to pay off each card and you'll pay a total of $295 in interest.

And if you can switch to a lower-rate card and increase your payments, you'll escape from the debt even faster. If you can get a 4 percent rate on each card and still pay $500 per month, you'll get out of debt after 11 months and only pay $94 in interest on each card.

It may be tough to come up with the extra money to pay down the cards, but at such a high rate this should be one of your top priorities. Continue to invest in your 401(k) up to the employer match, but divert any other extra money you've been investing—either for retirement or otherwise—to paying off the high-interest debt so you don't end up wasting any more money in interest payments.

If it's impossible to find much money to boost your payments, see if you can get help from a credit counseling agency. You can find an agency through the National Foundation for Credit Counseling (*www.nfcc.org*) or the Association of Independent Consumer Credit Counseling Agencies (*www.aiccca.org*). Also see the U.S. Trustee's list of approved credit counseling agencies, which have been vetted as a result of the new bankruptcy law (*www.usdoj.gov/ust*).

Your wife should also call the credit card companies and see if they'll offer her any special deals. She may be able to negotiate a settlement with the card companies by paying something like 55 cents on the dollar, but that will hurt her credit score.

Defaulting is the worst move because it can devastate your wife's record. Lenders can sue her and obtain a judgment that, depending on the state, may allow them to freeze her bank accounts, tow away her car, garnish her wages, or put a lien on her home. The key is to get help before missing any payments.

With all the hype about and lists of credit counseling/debt management companies, are there some that are actually good and how does one go about finding the good ones?

There are some great credit counseling agencies, which can help you review your debts, set a budget, and negotiate with your creditors if you need to. If you've only been paying the minimum on your credit card(s), missing payments, or are having trouble digging out of debt, then meeting with a good credit counselor may finally help you shake off your money troubles.

But the quality can vary enormously from firm to firm. Some have been fined by the Federal Trade Commission and IRS for charging hidden fees, misrepresenting their nonprofit status, and offering questionable advice that helps the creditors more than the people who sought counseling.

There is, however, a good resource that can help you find a reputable credit counseling agency. As part of the sweeping bankruptcy law that went into effect in late 2005, people must receive credit counseling from an approved agency within six months of filing for bankruptcy.

The U.S. Trustee's office (part of the Department of Justice) has been vetting credit-counseling agencies and lists approved firms on its Web site (*www.usdoj.gov/ust*). The Web site also includes the agencies' contact information, Web site information, and whether they do business in person, over the phone, or through the Internet. Even if you're nowhere near filing for bankruptcy, this resource can help you find a reputable counselor that can help you get your finances back on track.

With so many agencies to choose from, you'll need to do some additional research yourself. A good agency should charge $50 or less (budget counseling sessions generally cost less than $20), meet with you for 60 to 90 minutes, review your situation, and offer budgeting advice as the first step.

Beware of agencies that put too much pressure on signing up for a debt management program, where you pay all your bills to the agency and they pay your creditors. These programs can help some people, but aren't always the best solution, and some agencies focus on them too much because they're paid by the creditors to sign people up.

You can also search for credit counseling agencies through their two major trade associations: the National Foundation for Credit Counseling (*www.nfcc.org*) and the Association of Independent Consumer Credit Counseling Agencies (*www.aiccca.org*).

For more advice about finding a credit counseling agency, and problems with some firms, see the Federal Trade Commission's advice for choosing a credit counselor (*www.ftc.gov*).

I know that many of the bankruptcy laws changed at the end of 2005. Will you be forced to give money in your IRA or 529 accounts if you file for bankruptcy?

No. The 2005 bankruptcy law made it much more difficult to file for bankruptcy—requiring credit counseling and debtor education, making it tougher to keep your house, lengthening the period you have to wait before filing again, and making it much more difficult to discharge your debts by filing

Chapter 7, especially if you earn more than the median income in your state (generally about $40,000 per year for a family of four).

Even though the new law made it tougher to keep many assets, it made it easier to protect your IRA and a lot of money in your 529 account. The law clarified that IRAs—like 401(k)s—can't be touched even if you file Chapter 7 bankruptcy; however, you must use most of your other assets to pay off creditors. The new law caps the IRA protection at $1 million per person for money you've invested directly into the IRA, but the cap doesn't apply to money that was rolled over from 401(k)s or other pension plan.

The new law also clarifies the rules for 529s. You can keep an unlimited amount of money that you invested in a 529 two years ago or more, and can keep up to $5,000 that you invested more than one year but less than two years ago. But money that you invested in a 529 account within the past year is not considered an exempt asset, which means that you may need to use it to pay creditors if you file Chapter 7.

For more information, see the Nolo Press bankruptcy page (*www.nolo.com*), which does a great job of explaining the rules.

How to Fight Identity Theft

Every week I hear about a security breach that could lead to identity theft, and sometimes it's from big companies with which I've done business. What can I do to make sure my identity doesn't get stolen?

The frequent security breaches show how easily your personal information can be stolen even if you've made big efforts to protect yourself.

Here's what you should do if you've been affected by a security breach:

- Monitor your credit card statements and contact your card company immediately if you find any suspicious charges. Check your balances online, so you don't need to wait for the monthly statement to arrive. If your statement doesn't arrive in the mail one month, contact the card company just to make sure that an identity thief hasn't replaced your address with his.
- Check your credit report frequently. You can order a free copy of your report from each of the three credit bureaus every year at AnnualCreditReport.com. Stagger your requests so you'll get one free report every four months.
- Some security breaches are more dangerous than others. If your Social Security number and name are stolen, contact the three credit bureaus (Experian, Equifax, and TransUnion) and put a fraud alert on your account, which requires lenders to verify your identification before extending credit in your name. The initial fraud alert lasts 90 days and entitles you to a free credit report from each of the bureaus.
- If your ID is stolen, call the Federal Trade Commission's ID Theft Hotline (877-438-4338) and visit the FTC's identity theft Web site (*www.ftc.gov/idtheft*), which includes instructions for reporting ID theft. Fill out the identity theft affidavit to close your existing accounts that ID thieves have used or new fake accounts that have been opened in your name.
- File a report with your local police. Get a copy of the report (or at least the number) and send it to your creditors.
- For more advice, see the Identity Theft Resource Center (*www.idtheftcenter.org*) and the Privacy Rights

Clearinghouse (*www.privacyrights.org*), which includes details about many of the breaches.

Mutual fund firms are pushing hard to get customers to sign up for online access to their accounts. But what if someone hacks into my account and empties it? Would I have any legal recourse to require the mutual fund company to reimburse me for the loss?

To put it bluntly, no. You generally don't have any recourse unless you can prove that the institution was negligent in the theft.

But that doesn't mean you shouldn't do business on the Internet. Fund companies and brokers have gone to great lengths to protect your money online, both by encryption technology and by administrative procedures that would make it tough for someone to clean out your account.

At T. Rowe Price, for example, proceeds are sent only to the address you have on record. So if somebody were to hack into your account, the check would still show up at your address and be payable to you. If an address change is submitted online, the company does not allow redemptions for ten business days and sends a confirmation of the change to both the new and the old addresses.

Charles Schwab and E*Trade are among a handful of online brokerages that offer a security guarantee, promising to cover 100 percent of any losses in your account because of unauthorized activity. But those guarantees aren't ironclad. At Schwab, for instance, there's a key disclaimer: "If you share [your login or password] with anyone, we'll consider their activities to have been authorized by you."

Even if you're found to be at fault, you may still be able to get your money back. There have been cases where brokerage firms ended up making the customer whole, even though the client hadn't installed security software on his computer, such as spyware protection, because the firms figured that the bad PR associated with the incident would be worse than the money it cost to reimburse the customer.

New Rules for Student Loans

I know that the rules for student loan rates changed a lot in July 2006. Is it still worthwhile to consolidate my student loans?

It depends on when you took out the loans. The new rules now set fixed rates for new Stafford and PLUS loans taken out in 2006—Staffords now charge a fixed rate of 6.8 percent and parents pay 8.5 percent on PLUS loans.

But the rates on older Stafford loans and PLUS loans continue to be variable, changing each July 1 based on the 91-day Treasury-bill yield set the last Thursday in May. On July 1, 2006, those rates changed to be 6.5 percent during the grace period for Stafford loans, 7.1 percent afterward; and 7.9 percent for PLUS loans. But you can consolidate and lock in those rates; the consolidation rates are based on the weighted average of your loans, rounded up to 1/8 of a percent. Consolidating can also enable you to extend the repayment period on the loan, which can lower your monthly payment. Some lenders offer rebates or discounts in exchange for timely payments.

To run the numbers for your situation, see FinAid .org's Loan Consolidation Calculator.

When is student loan debt tax deductible?

The rules for deducting student loan interest were pretty strict in the past; you could only write off the interest you paid in the first five years, and only if your income was quite low. But the time frame and income limits expanded a few years ago. Now you can deduct up to $2,500 in student loan interest every year as long as your income is below certain cut-offs—$110,000 if married; $55,000 if single for 2007 (the deduction amount gradually phases out until your income reaches $140,000 for married couples; $70,000 for singles). You don't need to itemize to take the deduction. If you're in the 25 percent bracket, taking the maximum deduction will lower your tax bill by $625.

Your Home

Chapter 5

For many families, their home is their biggest investment—especially after the big run-up in prices over the past few years—and their greatest source of tax breaks. But it's also their largest debt and can generate a lot of extra expenses. With so much focus on the housing market over the past few years, mortgage companies started to offer many new options that can either make it easier to get into a new home or get in over your head.

Our readers are always asking about strategies to make the most of this giant investment, whether it's picking the best mortgage, qualifying for the lowest rates, avoiding hidden fees, making the most of tax breaks, or figuring out when to go ahead and buy the house or when it's better to wait. And their biggest question is about paying down their mortgage early: when is it worthwhile to devote extra cash to their house payments or invest it somewhere else?

Knowing the rules can give you a great opportunity to build up equity for your future, and it can shave a lot of money off one of your largest monthly expenses.

How Much Can You Afford and How Will You Pay for It?

I'd like to buy a new home in a few years but am wondering what goal I should shoot for. I currently earn $50,000 per year. How much home can I afford?

Instead of comparing the cost of the home to your annual income, it's more important to consider how much you've saved for a down payment, what kind of borrowing terms you can get, and how much equity you have in any house you sell to roll into a new one. A first-time homebuyer who has saved $10,000 for a down payment can't afford nearly as much as someone who has $80,000 in profit from the sale of their first home to put down—even if they both earn $50,000 per year.

All of these factors will affect your monthly payment, which is what lenders care about the most.

Lenders like for borrowers' monthly mortgage obligation (principal, interest, taxes, and homeowners' insurance) not to exceed 30 percent of their monthly gross income. And they usually want your total monthly debt service, which includes all of your loan payments including your mortgage, not to exceed 40 to 45 percent of your monthly gross income. Some lenders limit it to about 36 percent of your gross pay.

But just because lenders will give you that much money doesn't mean it's always a good idea to take it. Lenders are looking primarily at your other loans, but you also have to consider other expenses that affect your cash flow. And think about any circumstances that could change. If you're both working now but one of you would like to cut back after having kids, or if your job is not too stable, be very careful before committing to a payment that you couldn't continue to afford if your income situation changed.

My wife and I just got married and we'd like to buy a house soon. We've been setting aside money for the down payment but we have quite a ways to go; we'd need about $70,000 to make a 20 percent down payment in our area. We're wondering whether we should just go ahead and buy a house now with no money down or wait until we've saved the 20 percent?

Lenders are making it a lot easier to buy a house without the traditional 20 percent down payment. But you're going to pay a lot for that option. If you borrow more than 80 percent of the home's value, you'll usually have to pay private mortgage insurance, which protects the lender if you default on your loan. That tends to cost .5 percent to 1 percent of the loan value, which could cost $3,500 per year on a $350,000 home, or $5,000 on a $500,000 home. It's money that doesn't go toward your principal or interest and isn't tax deductible.

Another option is to piggyback two loans. If you take out one loan for 80 percent of the cost and another for 20 percent (or for 15 percent and pay 5 percent in a down payment), you can avoid PMI, and the interest on both loans is generally tax deductible, but the rates on that second loan are quite high—now running in the low to mid-9 percent range.

If you wait to amass the 20 percent down payment, you can avoid these extra costs, qualify for a lower-rate loan, and you'll keep your mortgage payments much lower, which gives you a lot more flexibility in the future if, for example, one of you wants to cut back on work after the kids are born. If your rent is reasonable and the housing market in your area has slowed, there's even less reason to rush into buying.

In a slow housing market, it's particularly important to put down 20 percent, so you have some equity in case you do have to move earlier than expected. The equity in your home can also give you an extra source of cash in an emergency.

I would like to cash out my IRA or my 401(k) to buy a single-family home. Can I do this when I am not a first-time homebuyer?

Perhaps. Surprisingly, the IRS defines a first-time homebuyer as someone who hasn't owned a home for the past two years, even if you owned one before then. If you sold your first home, then rented for a while, you could still get some tax benefits when you buy your next home.

In that case, you can withdraw up to $10,000 from a traditional IRA penalty free to buy or build a first home for you, your children, your grandchildren, or your parents. You'll still owe taxes on your earnings, just no penalty for early withdrawal.

If you have a Roth IRA, you can withdraw your contributions tax and penalty free anytime for any reason. You can also withdraw up to $10,000 of your earnings without taxes or penalties for a first home if you've held the Roth for at least five years.

In both cases, the $10,000 is per person—each spouse can withdraw $10,000 from an IRA for the home purchase. But the $10,000 is a lifetime limit; once you've withdrawn that much for a home, you can't take out any more money penalty free for a home purchase, even if you qualify as a first-time homebuyer again in the future.

The rules for IRA withdrawals are much more lenient than they are for 401(k)s. If you take money from your 401(k) to buy a home, you'll have to pay income taxes on it, plus a 10 percent penalty if you quit before age 55. But a little two-step will let you dodge part of the penalty. Roll the money into an IRA first, and then tap the account for your down payment. That way you can take the $10,000 from the IRA penalty free (although you will still owe tax on the withdrawal).

But there's a huge downside to raiding your retirement funds for your house. To access the money, you must withdraw it from the IRA accounts forever. You can't put the money back in later, which means you lose the ability to have tax-deferred—or tax-free—growth for years until retirement. Finding another source of money for the down payment now could help you protect thousands of dollars in future retirement savings.

When I bought my house, I only put 10 percent down and had to buy private mortgage insurance, which I hoped would be dropped soon after the value of my house increased. But it now looks like the housing market is starting to slow down in my area. What's this going to do to my efforts to get my PMI dropped?

It all depends on what already happened to housing values in your area since you first bought your property.

Most lenders require you to buy private mortgage insurance if your loan is for more than 80 percent of the house's value, and they generally charge from .5 percent to 1 percent of the loan value in annual premiums, adding up to $2,500 to $5,000 per year on a $500,000 mortgage, for example. These premiums aren't tax deductible and don't add to the equity of your home, but they can often be eliminated after your house increases in value.

Lenders are generally required to drop private mortgage insurance after your equity in your home reaches 22 percent of the property's value. But there's a big catch: in figuring your equity, the lender doesn't have to count any appreciation in value, only your down payment and the principal portion of your monthly payments. If you only put down 10 percent, it can take years before your equity reaches 22 percent of the property's value at the time you took out the mortgage.

But you don't have to wait for the lender to drop your PMI. The rules tend to be a lot more lenient if you ask the lender to drop the PMI instead of waiting for it to be dropped automatically. Many lenders will drop your PMI when your equity reaches at least 25 percent based both on your principal payments plus rising property values and any home improvements. They'll generally want an appraisal, which tends to cost about $250.

Lenders generally will not drop your PMI if you've missed any payments, and many require you to have the loan for at least two years first. If you refinance, you may be able to get rid of PMI because the new loan will be based on your house's current value.

Finding the Best Deal on Your Mortgage

I've been shopping around to refinance my mortgage and I keep seeing companies that offer loans with no closing costs. That sounds like a great deal, but is it too good to be true?

Those loans are worth looking into, but you need to ask a lot of questions. In most cases, having no closing costs doesn't really mean you won't have to pay any money at closing. Instead, it usually means that there aren't any lender fees; however, you'll still have to pay for title insurance, title search, appraisal, credit check, and other charges. Ask the lender for a good-faith estimate, which will list all of the fees it expects to charge. The exact numbers can change before closing, but at least you'll see what charges you'll still need to pay.

Lenders that offer low fees often make up the difference by charging a higher interest rate, so you need to look at all three parts of the equation: interest rate, fees, and points. Paying low fees can be most valuable if you only plan to keep the loan for a short period of time; a low interest rate is the most important if you expect to keep the house for a while. Run your numbers through the "Which Lender Has the Better Loan?" calculator at Kiplinger.com to see which offer works best for you.

Be sure to compare several offers. If the lender has a great rate but is charging high fees, see what you can negotiate down; they're more likely to cut you a deal if you have a good credit score or are taking out a large loan. And be sure to contact your current mortgage company, which may offer to match the competition to keep your business. You may also get a break on some of the closing costs, especially if the lender can use your old appraisal (usually only if it's no more than six months old) and offer you a reissue rate on your title insurance, which can save you a few hundred dollars.

For more information about the rights you have as a homebuyer and borrower, including the types of fees that lenders can charge, see the U.S. Department of Housing and Urban Development's Web site (*www.hud.gov*)—especially the section about settlement costs and information.

I'm about to buy a house and can really lower my monthly payment by taking an adjustable-rate mortgage (ARM) rather than a fixed one. But I'm worried that this might be a bad idea because interest rates are rising. What do you think?

I t all depends on how long you expect to live in the house. You can save a significant amount of money in monthly payments if you go with an ARM, and you won't have to worry about rising interest rates as long as you move before the rate rises on the ARM.

With a hybrid 5/1 ARM, for example, your rate is fixed for the first five years and then adjusts annually. If you move before five years, you never need to worry about what happens to rates and you may save a lot of money in interest—and maintain much lower payments. But if you stay in the house longer than five years and interest rates rise during that time, you run the risk that you'll get stuck with a much higher interest rate—and a much higher payment—than you would have had with the 30-year loan.

Find out exactly how the rate can rise: what index it's tied to, how quickly the rate can adjust after the fixed period is over (some inch up annually, but others move every six months or even monthly), and the maximum increase over the life of the loan. Figure out how high it can jump at the end of the fixed term, as well as the worst-case scenario.

If there's a chance you might still be in your house after five years, consider a hybrid 7/1 ARM instead, which locks in the rate for seven years in return for a moderately higher interest rate. Check out the mortgage page at Kiplinger.com to compare rates for your options. A 10-year ARM is rarely worth it because the rates are usually almost as high as they are for a 30-year loan.

I already have an adjustable-rate mortgage and the rate is about to rise. What should I do?

Homeowners whose adjustable-rate mortgages (ARM) are about to rise may still be better off keeping the loan rather than switching to a fixed rate. It all depends on how long you expect to live in the house.

If you'll be moving soon and can afford to make higher payments in the meantime, it might be worthwhile to stay put. You'll avoid refinancing costs and a prepayment penalty for getting out of your ARM. Even after the first adjustment, some ARM rates are still lower than current fixed rates.

But if you think you'll be in your home for a while, you may want to compare your current rate—and possible future increases—to a fixed rate mortgage or a hybrid ARM with a longer period before the rate adjusts, such as seven or ten years. Current rates on long-term loans are still reasonable, and there isn't a big risk to locking in the fixed loan. If rates go up, you looked smart by locking in. And if rates go down, you could always refinance. Run the numbers through the mortgage refinance calculator ("Refinancing an ARM into a FRM," listed as calculator 3e) at *www.mtgprofessor.com*.

How much of a difference can my credit score make in the interest rate I can get on a mortgage?

Your credit score can make a giant difference in your mortgage rate.

There are several types of credit scores, but most mortgage lenders use the FICO score to determine your credit risk. The median FICO score is 723, with most lenders requiring a score of at least 760 to get the best rates (the highest score is 850, but only 13 percent of people's scores beat 800).

Having a high score can save you thousands of dollars each year. A person with a FICO score of 760 or better could qualify for an average interest rate of 6.1 percent on a 30-year fixed-rate mortgage in late 2006. The average rate rose to 7.69 percent, however, for people with FICO scores of 620 to 639, according to Fair Isaac, the company that created the FICO scores most lenders use. That translates to higher payments of $229 per month, or $1,248 per year on a $216,000, 30-year mortgage.

And you'll take an even bigger hit if your score drops below 620. At that point, lenders often throw you into the subprime category, which can result in a rate that is 3 percent to 6 percent over someone with a better credit score. Visit Fair Isaac's myFICO.com Web site for more details about how your score can affect your rate and daily rate updates.

Your score can make an even bigger difference in the interest rates on home-equity lines of credit. Those rates tend to fall into 20 or 30 point buckets, where the interest rate for someone with a 670 score may be half a point higher than one with a 700, for example.

Your credit score also affects the rate you pay for private mortgage insurance, the amount of documentation your lender requires when you apply for a loan, the size of your down payment, the type of loan you can get, and the size of the loan. In some cases, for example, someone with a 700 or 660 score won't be able to borrow as much as someone with a higher score.

Your income, assets, and employment, which aren't considered in your credit score, can also affect your mortgage rate and the amount of the loan. But lenders often start with a credit-score cutoff for certain rates. If the cutoff is 700 and your score is 697, you won't qualify no matter how good the rest of your file looks.

What steps should I take to improve my credit score if I want to buy a house in the next year or so?

First, check your credit record with all three credit bureaus and have any errors corrected. You'll have a separate credit score based on your credit record from each of the major credit bureaus (Experian, Equifax, and TransUnion). Mortgage lenders usually get all three FICO scores and use the middle one. You can order a free credit report (but not a free score) from each of those three bureaus every 12 months at AnnualCreditReport.com. Or you can buy all three reports and FICO scores from MyFico.com, which is a good idea to do at least six months before buying a house.

When you get your score, go to MyFico.com to see how it can affect your mortgage rate, and how much of a difference improvements in your score can make.

Then, do everything possible to keep your score clean. Make big efforts to pay your bills on time and pay down any large credit card debts or other revolving accounts if you can, because high balances will hurt your credit rating. Also, don't open any new accounts.

It will also be beneficial to keep your account balances low for a while. The amount you've borrowed is what counts in your score, not how much you pay. The lender looks at your credit amount as a snapshot in time, whether or not you plan to pay off the entire bill immediately. It's best to keep your balances at 25 percent or less than your available credit. And don't close any old cards; lowering your available credit without lowering your total balance can hurt your credit score.

For more tips on improving your score, see the credit score section of Chapter 4, Credit and Debt.

We recently shopped for a home loan and got a credit analysis from Equifax. We disagree with two factors listed in the report. One was a delinquency that we know is incorrect because we always pay our bills on time and have never had a late fee. The report also said we had too many accounts with balances. But we have only two active credit cards and we pay them in full each month. How can we get these discrepancies cleared up quickly?

Credit bureaus can generally take up to 30 days to investigate disputes with consumers. But we'll let you in on a little secret: your mortgage lender might be able to get your report fixed in as little as 36 to 72 hours.

Lenders generally work with independent credit-reporting agencies, which gather information from the big-three credit bureaus (Equifax, Experian, and Trans-Union). Most of these middlemen also offer "rescoring" services, working with the credit bureaus to fix errors on your report within a few days and rerunning your score to reflect a more accurate risk factor, which can lower your rate and save you thousands of dollars in interest charges.

The process is labor intensive, so it's available only for mortgages, not smaller loans. And you can't do it on your own. You need to work through your lender, who will have to pay a rescoring fee—generally about $120 for two accounts corrected by two bureaus. As a result, you may have to lobby a reluctant lender to rescore your application.

Rescoring works only with legitimate errors, so you must provide documentation that the information is incorrect. In your case, you should be able to fix the delinquency error. But the balance issue may not be a mistake. Your credit score is based on how much you owe at the time the account is checked—even if you plan to pay the bill in full by the due date. Having too high a balance could hurt your score even if you end up paying off the entire amount the following day.

Should I Make Extra Payments?

My grandmother died and we just received about $20,000. We're wondering whether we should use the money to pay down our mortgage or whether we should invest it instead.

These days, there's rarely any reason to rush to pay off the mortgage. If you locked in low rates over the past few years, then you can generally do better by investing the money.

The key is to compare your after-tax interest rates. Paying down a mortgage with a 5.75 percent rate, for example, is the same as an investment that earns 5.75 percent. And if you're deducting the mortgage interest in the 25 percent bracket, a 5.75 percent mortgage really costs you just 4.3 percent after the tax benefits (although you may have to pay taxes on your investment, too). You can stretch the money even further if you add it to your 401(k), especially if you haven't been getting the full employer match, or use it to max out your Roth IRA, which gives you tax-free money for retirement.

Two other reasons to invest the money rather than paying down the mortgage are leverage and liquidity.

You already benefit from all of the home's price appreciation, whether you have 10 percent or 100 percent equity. And money you keep outside of the mortgage is much easier to access. Paying more toward your mortgage one month does not give you any more flexibility to make lower payments in future months—it just helps you pay off the loan earlier, which still may be more than a decade away. After you use that money to make extra payments, you won't be able to touch it again unless you take out a home equity loan or sell the house. On the other hand, if you invest the money, it's generally easier to access if you do lose your job or have an emergency and need the extra cash to make future mortgage payments.

Before deciding whether to invest the money or add it to your mortgage, first make sure your other financial bases are covered. Most important: pay off high-interest credit card debt. As soon as you stop paying high interest charges each month, you'll have more money to devote to other goals, which will have a huge ripple effect on the rest of your finances. Then beef up your emergency fund. You should keep three to six months' worth of living expenses in a safe and liquid account, so you won't have to go into debt or raid long-term savings for unexpected bills.

Even if you decide that it's better financially to invest the money, you might be comfortable using some of it to boost your mortgage payments too, which can shave some years off your loan and make a big difference in your retirement-spending calculations if you're nearing retirement and close to paying off the mortgage.

*I'm about to get a raise of $500 per month
and I'd like to use the extra money to help pay
down my mortgage. I bought a house last year,
borrowing $200,000 at 6 percent for a 30-year
fixed mortgage. If I add $500 per month to my
payments, how much quicker will I pay off my
house?*

Increasing your payments by $500 per month could make a huge difference in your mortgage. With a 30-year $200,000 mortgage at 6 percent, you're probably paying about $1,199 per month not counting any escrow for property taxes and homeowners' insurance. If you add the $500—bringing your monthly payment to $1,699—you'll pay off your house in just under 15 years, cutting the term of your mortgage nearly in half. And you'll save big money in interest, paying just $103,249 instead of $231,676. Run your numbers through the "How Advantageous Are Extra Payments?" calculator at Kiplinger.com to see how much you can save.

It's better to add the payments to your mortgage yourself rather than signing up to have a service do it; those services generally charge high fees for the same thing you can do yourself. And by adding the money on your own, you don't always have to pay the extra $500 every month, giving you the option to use the money elsewhere without penalty if you have an emergency or cut down on the extra payments if you lose your job.

Paying off your house early can help your financial situation, especially if you're nearing retirement age. But make sure the rest of your finances are in order before you devote the extra money to extra mortgage payments, especially if you have a low interest rate. First pay off high-interest credit card debts, save three to six months' worth of living expenses in a liquid emergency fund, and max out your 401(k), especially if you have an employer match. And with your low interest rate, you may decide that it's better to invest some of the money rather than use it to pay off the house.

The Tax Benefits of Homeownership

What house-related expenses can we write off on our taxes?

You get a lot of tax breaks when you own a home, which makes homeownership a bit more affordable. The biggest is the tax deduction for mortgage interest. You can write off the interest on up to $1 million in debt to buy or substantially improve your first or second home (interest on a mortgage for a third home is not deductible unless it is a business or rental property).

The deductible interest can give you big savings at tax time—especially in the early years of owning the home, when most of your payments go toward interest. If you just took out a $500,000 mortgage and are paying 6.5 percent interest on a 30-year loan, your monthly payments are $3,160. In the first year, about $2,600 to $2,700 of each payment goes toward interest (the amount decreases slightly each month), while the rest goes toward principal. By the end of the first year, you should have paid $32,335 in interest. If you're in the 28 percent tax bracket, those interest payments could cut your tax bill by $9,053. Run the numbers through the "How Much Will My Home Payments Be?" calculator at Kiplinger.com (then click the "Tables" tab) to see how much interest you'll be able to write off each year.

You can also write off your property taxes annually and the points paid in the year you bought the house, even if the home seller paid them for you. If you paid two points (each point is 1 percent of the loan) on a $500,000 loan, you could write off $10,000 in the year you buy the house, which could lower your tax bill by up to $2,800 if you're in the 28 percent bracket. You can also deduct the points you paid when you refinance, but you must spread that deduction over the life of the loan. So if you refinance to a new 30-year $500,000 loan and pay for two points, you need to spread that $10,000 write-off over the 30-year term of the loan, letting you deduct $333 per year. If you sell the house before you pay off the loan—or if you refinance again before paying off the loan—then you can deduct the remainder in the year that you sell or refinance.

You can't deduct closing costs in the year you buy the house, but you can use them to increase your cost basis if you have a tax bill when you sell (see below for the tax rules on home sale profits). You can also use the cost of major home improvements to increase your tax basis when you sell.

You also can deduct the interest on up to $100,000 in home-equity debt every year—no matter what you use the money for—which can give you a low-interest alternative to a car loan or student loan, as long as you make sure that you can afford to continue to make the payments so you don't put your house at risk.

I recently sold my house for $370,000. I made a profit of $127,000. I owned the house for over three years. I'm looking to put $100,000 down on a new house. Do I have to pay capital gains taxes on any of my profits?

Nope. Most people don't owe taxes on their home sale profits, and you probably won't either, even if you don't end up buying a new house. As long as you've owned and lived in the house for two out of the past five years, single people can exclude $250,000 in profits from taxes when they sell the house; married couples can exclude $500,000. A married couple who bought a house for $200,000, for example, could sell it for up to $700,000 without having to pay capital gains taxes.

If you haven't lived in the house for two years, then you'll generally need to pay capital gains taxes on your profits (long-term gains of up to 15 percent if you've owned the house for more than a year; short-term gains, in your income-tax bracket, if you've had it for less than a year).

You can exclude part of your profits in certain circumstances, such as if you move because of a new job that is at least 50 miles farther away from your old home than your old job was, if you must move because of your health or the health of relatives in your care, or if you are affected by other unforeseen circumstances approved by the IRS, including death, divorce, becoming eligible for unemployment compensation, multiple births from the same pregnancy, damage to the home from a natural or man-made disaster or an act of war or terrorism, and a few other reasons.

In that case, you can prorate the exclusion based on the amount of time you lived in the house. If you lived there for one year and have to move because of a new job, for example, then you can exclude $125,000 from taxes if you're single, $250,000 for married couples (half the full exclusion because you lived there for one year, which is half the two-year limit). You can also lower your tax bill by adding closing costs and the cost of major home improvements to your tax basis.

What are the tax implications for an unmarried couple that sells a house? We've lived in the house for more than 20 years and never rented it out. We've split the mortgage, property-tax bill, and income-tax deduction.

If you're both listed on the title, you can each exclude up to $250,000 of your profits from capital gains taxes. That's the amount of the profit that single individuals can exclude from taxes if they've lived in a house for at least two out of the past five years.

If you own the house jointly and sell it for $400,000 more than you paid for it, for example, you'll each have $200,000 in profits—well within the $250,000 capital gains exclusion. If you sell the house for a $600,000 profit, you'll each owe tax on a $50,000 gain.

I have been married for over two years and my wife lives with me in the home we plan to sell. Do we qualify for the $500,000 tax-free gain on our home? The deed is in my name only.

As long as you've both lived in the house for at least two of the past five years, you should qualify for the $500,000 exclusion if you're married filing jointly, even though your wife isn't on the deed.

You can only take that full exclusion, however, if neither you nor your wife excluded the gain from the sale of another home within the past two years. This could happen, for example, if each spouse owned a home before they were married, then one sold their residence to move in with the other. If that happened, then that spouse would be ineligible for the exclusion, but the other spouse could still exclude $250,000 in profits, the same level available to single people.

Prior to putting our house on the market, we spent more than $9,000 on renovations and another $3,000 on repairs. Can we write off any of these expenses on our taxes?

P robably not. The cost of repairs has no tax impact, and the money you spent on renovations may not affect your tax bill, either. The only improvements that count for taxes on a personal home are changes that added to the house's value rather than simply maintained it in good shape, such as adding an addition to your home. But even then, the costs aren't tax-deductible. Instead, you can add them to your tax basis—along with the costs to buy the house—which can lower the taxable profit on the sale.

But that only matters if your gain on the sale exceeds $250,000 (or $500,000 if you're married and file a joint return). That much profit is tax free, assuming you owned and lived in the house for two of the five years leading up to the sale.

I refinanced my house for the second time last year and didn't realize that I could deduct the rest of the points I paid the last time I refinanced. Did I miss my chance or can I deduct these points on my next year's tax return?

A lot of people overlook this tax deduction, but you didn't miss your chance to take the write-off.
In the year that you buy a house, you can deduct the points you paid to get your loan, and even points the sellers paid on your behalf. If you pay points to refinance, though, you must spread the deduction over the life of the loan; so if you paid two points on a $200,000 loan, you'd be paying a total of $4,000. If

the loan were for 30 years, then you'd only be able to deduct $133 per year ($4,000 divided by 30).

But if you refinance again or sell your home, you can deduct the remaining points all in that year. If you refinance again after just one year, for example, you can deduct the remaining $3,867 ($4,000 minus $133) from the first time you refinanced.

Even if you forgot to take this deduction in the past, you can still reap the benefits now. You can't take the extra money on your next year's tax return; instead, you'll need to file an amended return. You have up to three years after the original due date of your return to file an amended return if you've made a mistake or left something out. To make the change, print out Form 1040-X ("Amended U.S. Individual Income Tax Return") from *www.irs.gov* and fill in the numbers from your original return and then add the changes you're making. You'll also need to submit a new Schedule A because you're changing your itemized deductions.

Tax Breaks for Landlords

I have two rental properties in addition to my home. Can I deduct the mortgage interest on the rental?

Sure. The interest paid on the rental properties is a business expense, just like property taxes, the cost of repairs, homeowners' insurance, maintenance, utilities, management fees, and depreciation.

If, after subtracting all those expenses from the rent you collected, you show a loss for the year, you may also be able to deduct up to $25,000 of that loss from other income, such as your salary. That write-off is available as long as you are actively involved in renting the properties and your adjusted gross income is less than

$100,000. The $25,000 deduction gradually disappears as your adjusted gross income moves up to $150,000.

I just sold a house that I owned for 13 years. I rented it for the past 11 years. What are my tax obligations?

The tax rules are a lot more complicated when you sell rental property than when you sell the house you live in—in which case the profit is almost always tax free. When you sell a rental, you probably owe tax on the profit, and figuring that profit can be very time-consuming. Among other things, you need to add up all the depreciation deductions you claimed during the 11 years you rented the place.

First, you need to establish your tax basis. That's basically what you paid for the house, plus the cost of capital improvements (a new roof or central air-conditioning, for example), minus all the depreciation deductions. You subtract the basis from the proceeds of the sale to find your profit.

Profit attributable to appreciation is taxed at 15 percent as a long-term capital gain. The part attributable to depreciation (every dollar used to reduce the basis for depreciation adds a dollar to the profit side of the ledger) is taxed at 25 percent.

You report the sale on Form 4797 and figure the tax bill on Schedule D, both of which are filed along with your Form 1040 in April. If the profit is significant, you may need to make quarterly estimated tax payments before then. For more information, see IRS Publication 523, "Selling Your Home," at *www.irs.gov*.

A few years ago, I converted my home into a rental. If I move back in and then sell the house, will I be able to avoid capital gains if I've lived in the house two years out of the previous five years?

Most of your profit will probably be tax free. To qualify for tax-free profit on a home sale (up to $250,000 if you're single, $500,000 if you're married and file a joint return), you must own and live in the house for at least two of the five years leading up to the sale. Living in the house both before and after the rental will count toward the 24 months you need.

This assumes that you did not buy and sell another place while you were renting out your home and use the capital gains exclusion. You must wait at least two years after you sell a house (and claim tax-free profit) before you can do it again.

But be aware that not all of your gain from the reconverted rental can be tax free. Profit attributable to depreciation while you rent out the house (depreciation cuts your basis and therefore increases profit dollar for dollar when you sell) will be taxed at a flat 25 percent.

Lower Your Taxes

Chapter 6

axes become much more interesting when you realize that it's an area in which you can save hundreds of dollars every year—but only if you know the rules. In fact, people tend to pay much more money in taxes than they need to just because they don't take all of the write-offs they deserve or make the most of some key strategies that can cut their bills significantly. I receive a lot of questions from readers asking for details about which deductions they can take, how the rules work, and frequently overlooked ways to save on their tax bill. Everyone can learn from their questions.

It's also a particularly good time to review your tax situation and look for additional ways to reduce your bill. Congress made some major changes to the tax laws over the past year, offering even more savings opportunities than were available in the past. Learning about the new laws is a great way to cut your costs, especially if you don't wait until April and scramble around at the last minute searching for receipts. Take some time now to figure out how to take advantage of all of these tax breaks, and then do some advance planning that can cut your bill even further in the future. The money is just sitting there waiting for you, but only if you know the strategies for tapping it.

What Can You Deduct?

Can I take the child care tax credit for sending my daughters to camp this summer?

Perhaps. The cost of day camp can qualify for the dependent care tax credit if your children are under age 13 and you're sending them to camp so you can work. You can also deduct the cost of daycare, preschool, a nanny, or other babysitter while you are working. If you're married, both you and your spouse must have earned income during the year.

The size of the credit depends on the number of children and your income. You can count up to $3,000 in child care expenses for one child, $6,000 for two children. Low-income families can take a credit for up to 35 percent of those expenses, and families earning more than $43,000 can deduct 20 percent. So, if you have two kids and pay more than $6,000 for preschool, a nanny, or day camp, you can claim a $1,200 credit if you earn more than $43,000.

To take the credit, you'll need to file IRS Form 2441 with your taxes, and you'll need to know the care provider's employer ID number. For more details about what qualifies and how much—especially if you work part-time or get child care benefits through work—see IRS Publication 503, "Child and Dependent Care Expenses," available at *www.irs.gov*.

My husband graduated from medical school a few months ago and we moved to California, where he's doing his residency. Can we deduct our moving expenses and his job-search costs from our taxes?

You can generally deduct moving expenses if your new job is at least 50 miles farther from your home than your old job. But for people starting their first job, the new workplace must be at least 50 miles from the old residence.

You'll be able to deduct the cost of packing, storage (within 30 days of the move), and hiring a moving company or renting a moving truck, as well as one-way travel expenses to your new home for everyone in the household. You don't need to itemize to deduct these expenses.

Unfortunately, you won't be able to deduct job-search expenses for your first job or if you're switching careers.

People who are changing jobs within the same line of work, however, can deduct the cost of printing and mailing resumes, job-hunting phone calls, employment-agency fees, and the cost of travel to attend job interviews, whether or not you end up getting that job. But those are considered miscellaneous itemized deductions (like employee business expenses and investment-related expenses), which means you can only take the deduction if you itemize and you can only take the deduction after those expenses exceed 2 percent of your adjusted gross income.

There are, however, a few other expenses that your husband can probably deduct. State medical licensing fees, dues paid to professional associations, and the cost of books and other materials needed to perform his job are deductible. But these employee business expenses are also considered miscellaneous itemized deductions and are subject to the 2 percent adjusted gross income threshold (the rules are different for self-employed people). For more details about these write-offs, see IRS Publication 529, "Miscellaneous Deductions," available at *www.irs.gov.*

It looks like I am just a few hundred dollars over the cutoff for the 15 percent tax bracket (I'm single and earn $43,000). Is there anything I can do to quickly take me back? I am a teacher and a single mother of two teenage kids, with no support whatsoever, so it is quite a loss for me.

There's good news for you: the tax brackets are actually a tiered system, which means that only the amount of money above each cutoff is taxed at the higher rate. For people filing as head of household in 2007, for example, the first $11,200 in taxable income is taxed at 10 percent, then money earned from $11,201 to $42,650 is taxed at 15 percent, and any earnings from $42,651 to $110,100 is taxed at the 25 percent rate.

So, if you do have $43,000 in taxable income, you'll only pay the 25 percent tax rate for the $350 above the $42,650 limit (adding only $87.50 to your tax bill), and the rest of your money will be taxed at the 10 percent and 15 percent rates.

Also keep in mind that this only applies to taxable income; you'll be able to subtract exemptions and deductions before then, and money you contribute to a 401(k), 403(b), or flexible spending account can also lower your taxable income. You'll also be able to subtract several tax credits directly from your tax bill, such as $2,000 in child credits and any child care tax credits you can receive, whether or not you itemize.

Under what circumstances can you deduct medical expenses from your taxes?

You can only deduct medical expenses that weren't covered by insurance or tax-advantaged plans such as a flexible spending account or a health savings account. And you still may not be able to take the deduction even if you have a slew of expenses that qualify; you must itemize your deductions and can only write off medical expenses after they exceed 7.5 percent of your adjusted gross income. That means if you're earning $50,000 per year, you can only deduct out-of-pocket medical expenses beyond $3,750, leaving you with a deduction of just $1,250 on $5,000 of qualified costs.

But even that partial deduction can still make a difference. If you're in the 25 percent bracket, a $1,250 deduction can lower your tax bill by $313. It's worthwhile to keep the receipts in your tax file throughout the year because you could end up with a surprisingly large deduction if you have a medical emergency or a major expense that isn't covered by insurance, such as fertility treatments, orthodontia, laser eye surgery, or any experimental medical procedures that your insurer won't touch.

Once you pass that threshold, you can write off other nonreimbursed expenses that are usually too small to qualify, such as dental treatment, eye exams, contact lenses, glasses, a portion of your premiums for qualified long-term care insurance policies (the amount varies by age), prescription drugs not covered by insurance, the cost of transportation to receive medical care (20 cents per mile in 2007 if you drive), and many other expenses. For a comprehensive list of deductible expenses, see IRS Publication 502, "Medical and Dental Expenses."

Even if you contribute the maximum to your flexible spending account at work—generally $2,000 to $3,000 per year—you still may have some leftover expenses to write off. If one year you spend $20,000 for two rounds of in vitro fertilization that isn't covered by your health insurance, and you pay for $3,000 of the cost from your flexible spending account, for example, then you'll still have $17,000 in nonreimbursed medical expenses that could qualify for the tax write-off. If you earn $60,000 per year, you can write off any medical expenses beyond $4,500 (7.5 percent of your adjusted gross income). That still leaves you with $12,500 to write off, which will lower your tax bill by $3,125 if you're in the 25 percent bracket.

My son was diagnosed with brittle bone disease. We will need to remodel our home to accommodate his needs. We will need to replace the tile flooring and widen the hallways to create wheelchair access and make the backyard accessible with ramps. Can I write off these expenses?

You can deduct the cost of remodeling you need to do because of your son's medical condition, but only to the extent that it doesn't increase the value of the home.

The IRS has determined that the costs to add ramps and support bars, as well as to widen hallways and doorways for a wheelchair, can be deducted in full as medical expenses. But some other expenditures, such as installing higher-quality flooring or an elevator, may add to your home's value; ask a real estate professional how much value it might add when determining how much you can deduct.

If, for example, remodeling costs a total of $50,000 but increases the value of your home by only $5,000, you can consider $45,000 a deductible medical expense. Add the remodeling costs to other nonreimbursed medical expenses, which are deductible only to the extent that they exceed 7.5 percent of your adjusted gross income, and only if you itemize. If you earn $100,000 and have $40,000 in medical expenses, you can deduct $32,500.

You may be able to include some medical expenses you may not have considered, such as travel for yourself and your son for medical purposes and the extra cost to modify a vehicle to accommodate a wheelchair. For a list of deductible medical expenses, see IRS Publication 502, "Medical and Dental Expenses."

Will families be able to deduct hurricane losses that are not covered by any type of insurance on their federal income-tax returns?

You generally can deduct nonreimbursed casualty losses, whether they're from any kind of storm or disaster. But you'll probably get less money back than you think. You can only deduct any part of the loss that hasn't been reimbursed by insurance, and then you generally need to subtract $100 and reduce the loss by 10 percent of your adjusted gross income (although the $100/10 percent rules were waived for victims of Hurricanes Katrina, Rita, and Wilma). Then you can deduct the remainder, if you itemize your taxes. You'll need to report the loss on IRS Form 4684.

You usually have to wait until you file your taxes the following April to take the deduction, but you'll have some additional options if the loss was considered to be in a federal disaster area. In that case, you generally have a choice of writing off the loss when you file next April or taking a retroactive deduction for last year's return, which gives you a refund without having to wait. To take the retroactive loss, you'll need to file an amended return, Form 1040-X, and write the name of the hurricane on top in red, so that the IRS will expedite your claim.

Because the loss is generally reduced by 10 percent of your adjusted gross income, you'll probably want to claim the write-off in the year in which your income is lower.

For help figuring out what you can deduct, see IRS Publication 547, "Casualties, Disasters and Thefts." The IRS's "Casualty, Disaster and Theft Loss Workbook" can help you assess and itemize the damage room by room.

Who is eligible for the Saver's Tax Credit?

The Saver's Tax Credit is one of the most frequently overlooked credits, and it's a great opportunity for people below a certain income level to get an extra bonus for contributing to a retirement plan.

Married couples earning less than $50,000 can get a tax credit of up to $2,000 for contributing to an IRA, 401(k), or other employer-sponsored retirement plan. Singles earning less than $25,000 can get a tax credit of up to $1,000. The specific amount of the write-off is calculated by multiplying your eligible contribution by the credit rate, which is based on your adjusted gross income. Married couples can count up to $4,000 in contributions to a traditional or Roth IRA, 401(k), simplified employee pension (SEP), SIMPLE IRA, 457, or 403(b); singles can count up to $2,000 in eligible contributions.

For example, a married couple earning $30,000 or less can receive a credit for 50 percent of their eligible contributions. Because they can only count up to $4,000 in contributions in the equation, they'll get a tax credit of up to $2,000. The credit rate falls to 20 percent for couples earning $30,000 to $32,500, and then 10 percent for those earning $32,501 to $50,000. In that case, a couple contributing $4,000 or more to their retirement plans could get a tax credit of $400.

This credit is not available to children under age 18 and full-time students, even if they open their own retirement accounts. But it's a great incentive for people who are just starting out in their first jobs after college and didn't think they could afford to save.

Taxes and Your Investments

I sold some stock earlier this year but haven't kept good records. How do I figure out my tax bill?

Your tax bill is usually based on the difference between the amount you sold the stock for and your tax basis. If you bought the stock yourself, your basis is what you paid for the shares including brokerage commissions (different rules apply if you inherited the stock or received it as a gift). If you have your old trade confirmations, it'll be easy to look up the amount of money you originally invested.

If you don't have that paperwork, then you'll have to take a few more steps to track down the cost. It's worthwhile to find out how much you paid; otherwise, you'll get stuck paying taxes on the total value when you sell the shares, rather than just on the earnings, leaving you with a much bigger tax bill than you should be paying.

Ask your broker for some help. Brokers must keep records for six years, and some go back further (although you may have to pay a small fee to receive a duplicate statement).

If your broker doesn't keep records that far back, try to remember when you bought the shares and see what they were selling for at the time. A stock certificate might be dated or old tax returns might show when you began reporting dividend income. Then look up historical price quotes. If you can narrow down the purchase period to a few months, use the average price during that time as your basis and keep records of your methodology. BigCharts.com is a great source for historical price information, but its records only go back to January 1985. You also can use a service such as Gains Keeper, which can calculate your basis and tax bill for you (go to *www.gainskeeper.com* for a 30-day free trial).

You may also find some helpful information at the investor relations page on the company's Web site. Some companies, such as AT&T, have a special Web page just for tax basis information, which includes a link to worksheets that can help you figure out your basis—a tricky task if the company has had any spin-offs or mergers since you bought the stock.

Things are much easier if you inherited the stock. In that case, your basis is generally the stock's value when your benefactor died.

Another option to keep in mind for the future: Before selling a stock with a tough-to-calculate basis, consider giving it away to a charity rather than giving cash. That way you'll never need to pay capital gains taxes (so you don't need to worry about finding out the basis), and you can deduct the current value of the stock when you give it as a charitable contribution, if you itemize.

I've got $12,500 in carryover capital losses (because I had more losses than I could deduct last year). I netted $35,000 in capital gains from the sale of stock earlier this year. Can I offset $12,500 of the $35,000?

Yes. The law allows you to use capital losses to offset capital gains dollar for dollar—first subtracting short-term losses from short-term gains (investments held one year or less), and then subtracting long-term losses from long-term gains (held longer than one year). You can then use any remaining losses to offset any remaining gains in the other category.

If you still had more losses than gains, you could also deduct up to $3,000 in losses against other kinds of income, such as your salary. Any losses beyond that are carried over to future years, where you can first use them to offset capital gains, and then, if you still have more losses left over, you can deduct up to $3,000 of any remaining losses from your income. You can continue this process every year until you've finally deducted all of your losses.

The only limit on how much carryover loss you can use in one year is how much gain you have to offset.

When you file your taxes, you'll need to report your capital gains and losses on Schedule D, which has a worksheet to help you with the calculations (available at *www.irs.gov*).

Can my husband and I write off $6,000 of stock losses each year if we file a joint return? And, if so, does the stock have to be owned in individual names rather than jointly?

It doesn't matter how you own the stock: you're stuck with the same $3,000 limit that applies to single people. Remember, capital losses can be deducted dollar for dollar against any amount of capital gains, and then up to $3,000 a year can be used to offset other kinds of income, such as salary or interest income. Any excess loss is carried over to future years.

And don't even think of trying to double your deduction by filing separate tax returns. That has all sorts of pitfalls for married couples, including a $1,500 limit on capital loss deductions.

I've received conflicting feedback from two CPAs regarding this issue: I have $25,000 in stock losses remaining as a result of liquidations last year. I closed on the sale of my primary residence (for the last five years) this year and I stand to incur capital gains beyond the $250,000 exemption for a single person. Can I use the carryover stock losses from last year to offset capital gains of this year's real estate sale?

Those bad stock picks will finally pay off. Yes, you can use the capital losses you carried over from last year to offset some of your home sale profits for this year.

As long as you've lived in your home for at least two of the past five years, you won't owe taxes on $250,000 of profits if you're single; $500,000 if you're married. Exceed that amount and you'll owe capital gains taxes on the additional profit. If you bought your house for $200,000 and sold it for $500,000, for example, you'll owe long-term capital gains taxes on the $50,000 in profit beyond the exclusion (because you're single).

As with stocks and mutual funds, the profit is considered a long-term capital gain if you've owned the house for more than a year. These gains are reported on Schedule D of your tax forms.

Long-term capital losses offset long-term capital gains, short-term losses offset short-term gains, and then any remaining losses can offset whatever type of gains are left. If your overall losses exceed your gains, you can deduct up to $3,000 of excess losses from other income (such as your salary) in one year, and then you must carry over the remaining losses to future years, when they can be used to offset capital gains.

And don't forget to take other steps to minimize your taxable gain on the sale of your home, such as add-

ing closing costs and the cost of certain home improvements (ones that add value to your home) to the cost
basis of your house. For more information, see Chapter
5, Your Home, and IRS Publication 523, "Selling Your
Home."

If I sell a stock for a loss to offset some gains, do I have to wait a certain period of time before I can rebuy that stock?

You generally can use your losses to offset any capital gains you have for the year, and then you can
use up to $3,000 of any additional losses to lower
your income (with any extra losses rolling over to help
with next year's tax bill).

But under the "wash sale" rule, you can't deduct the
loss if you buy the same stock within 30 days before or
after you sell it. So if you think the stock will eventually
rebound, it's a good idea to keep an eye on your calen-
dar before buying it back.

If you do buy the stock back within 30 days, though,
you don't lose the loss forever. A loss denied by the
wash sale rule is added to the cost basis of the newly
purchased shares. That will lower your tax bill when you
sell the new shares. For example, suppose you bought
100 shares of Fancy Stock for $1,000 and sold them for
$750. Less than 30 days later, you think Fancy Stock is
poised for a takeoff and you can't wait any longer to buy
100 shares at $800. You can't deduct the $250 loss in the
year of the wash sale, but you can add it to your basis.
When you finally sell Fancy Stock, your gain or loss will
be calculated from $1,050 ($800 plus $250).

My mother wants to give me some stock that she acquired many years ago. What would be my cost basis? Do I pay tax based on the value on the date I received the gift? The stock has appreciated over the years.

Determining the basis is usually simple when you're given a stock that has appreciated in value. In that case, your basis is the same as your mother's basis—generally the amount that your mother originally paid for the stock and any reinvested dividends (plus brokerage commissions).

You can also use your mother's holding period. Because your mother owned the stock for several years, you'll be taxed at long-term capital gains rates no matter when you sell—even if you only end up owning it for less than a year.

But gifting stock to a grown child can actually create a bigger tax bill than your mother would have had herself. If she's in a lower tax bracket than you are, it would be better if she sold the stock herself, paid capital gains taxes at her lower rate, and then gave you the cash (you can give up to $12,000 per person per year without being subject to gift taxes). People in the 10 and 15 percent income tax brackets only pay 5 percent in long-term capital gains taxes, and in 2008 to 2010, that long-term capital gains rate falls to 0 percent for people in those lowest two tax brackets. Everyone else pays 15 percent in long-term capital gains taxes.

Or you may be even better off tax-wise if she holds on to the stock and gives it to you after she dies (as long as she isn't worried about removing it from her estate now if she'd be subject to estate taxes). If you inherit the stock instead, your basis will generally be the value of the stock when your mother dies. This "step-up in basis" eliminates the tax bill on years of increases in the stock's value.

My brother wants to give me stock he bought for much more than its $10,000 value. When I sell, is my tax basis what he paid or the price on the day I receive it?

I hope you're sitting down because the answer is a doozy. It would be easy to calculate the capital gains bill if the stock had increased in value. In that case, your basis would be the amount that your brother had originally paid for the stock, plus any reinvested dividends and brokerage commissions.

But because the stock has declined in value, your basis depends on how much you get when you sell it. Let's assume your brother bought the stock for $20,000 and it's worth $10,000 at the time of the gift. If you sell for less than $10,000, your basis is the $10,000 date-of-gift value, so you can claim a tax loss equal to the decline in value after the gift. (No one gets a deduction for the drop in value before the gift.)

If you sell for more than $20,000, then $20,000 is your basis, and your profit is measured from that point. If you sell for between $10,000 and $20,000, you have neither a gain nor a loss. It might be best for your brother to sell the stock and claim the tax loss himself, and then give you $10,000 in cash.

And if you had inherited the stock instead, then your basis would generally be the stock's value on the day the person died.

I invested $12,000 in the late 1990s in Roth IRAs for my wife and myself. The value today is about $10,000. Will there be any penalty if I withdraw the money? I'm only 57 years old.

Only Roth earnings are taxable—not contributions—so you could withdraw the $10,000 without any penalty or tax bill, even though you're under age 59½.

And you may even be able to deduct your $2,000 loss. To do so, you'd need to close out all of your Roth IRA accounts and still have a loss.

Unlike other investment losses, however, IRA losses are considered a miscellaneous itemized deduction, which you can write off only if you itemize and only to the extent that those deductions are greater than 2 percent of your adjusted gross income.

I invested in a company that declared bankruptcy. Can I write off the loss as a worthless stock?

Not necessarily. Just because a company declares bankruptcy doesn't mean that the stock is automatically considered worthless. In fact, sometimes it continues to trade off a major stock exchange, perhaps for pennies per share on the Pink Sheets, and it may bounce back after bankruptcy.

In other cases, the company cancels that stock and issues a new one if it does emerge from bankruptcy, thus rendering the old shares worthless. If the company goes out of business entirely, the stock also may become worthless. When that happens, you can write off the loss as if the stock had $0 value. In the section of your tax forms where you have to report the sale date and selling price, just write "worthless." But you have to write off the loss in the year the stock became worthless, which isn't always obvious. If you miss taking the loss in that year, you have seven years to file an amended return to report a loss for a worthless stock (see *www.irs.gov* for Form 1040-X).

If you think a stock may be worthless, search the Internet and see if it's trading anywhere. Your broker may be able to help you search for its status. If the stock is still trading somewhere, even if it's only for a few pennies, you can't write it off as worthless. But you may still have a significant loss if you can sell the shares. Even if you can't sell them on the market, ask your broker what you can do. Sometimes a broker will buy them from you for $1 just so you can write off a loss on your taxes.

Kids and Taxes

My son will earn about $2,400 from his summer job. Will he need to file income taxes this year? If not, can he still contribute to a Roth IRA without filing income taxes? And if he contributes to a Roth IRA, can I still claim him as my dependent on my tax return because I still support him with food, insurance, travel expenses, etc.?

If your son's income was all earned from that job—not from any investments—then he'd only have to file a tax return if that earned income is more than $5,350 in 2007.

But if he also has more than $250 in income for the year from investments—including interest, dividends, or capital gains from a bank, mutual fund, or brokerage account in his own name, including custodial accounts—then he may need to file a return even if his earned income was less than $5,350. For details about the rules, check out the IRS's Taxes for Students page (*www.irs.gov/individuals/students/index.html*), which includes a flow chart that walks you through the requirements.

If he didn't have a job but only earned income from his investments, then he'd only need to file a return if he had more than $850 in investment income.

Even if he isn't required to file a tax return, it's a good idea to send in the paperwork if any income taxes were withheld from his paychecks; that's the only way he'll get that money back. (He'll only get back the income tax withheld; Social Security taxes are not refundable.)

He can still contribute up to his earned income (the $2,400) to a Roth IRA, whether or not he decides to file a tax return. And contributing to a Roth won't affect his status as a dependent.

It was a great idea to open a Roth IRA for him; it's a good way to learn about long-term savings, it can be a tremendous source of tax-free income in retirement (especially after having more than 40 years to grow!), and he can withdraw the contributions at any time tax and penalty free.

Even if he spends the $2,400 he earned, you can still contribute up to that amount to his Roth yourself. The key is that you can't contribute more than the amount of money he earned during the year from a job (investment income doesn't count). And unlike traditional IRA contributions, which are shown on tax returns to claim the deduction, Roth contributions are not reported to the IRS.

If your children earn money from lawn mowing or babysitting and you want to open up a Roth IRA for them, what documentation do you need to provide to the IRS in order to show that they have earned income?

That's a great idea to open a Roth IRA for your children; you'll give them a big head start on a tax-free retirement-savings fund. Children can only contribute up to the amount of their earned income for the year (with a maximum of $4,000 in 2007, like all adults under age 50). As long as they have the earned income, you can give them the money to make their contribution.

They don't need to file an income-tax return to qualify. But you do need to keep records for your own files proving that they did have earned income, in case you're audited in the future. Even if they're just doing occasional babysitting or yard work, keep track of the date of each job, the person who employed them, and how much they earned.

Some firms don't want to open up Roth IRAs for minors because they're worried about legal issues, but several brokerages, including Charles Schwab, T.D. Waterhouse, and Merrill Lynch, and mutual fund companies, such as T. Rowe Price, American Century, and Vanguard, will open the accounts for minors (although some require a parent's signature).

What are the tax rules if I give my kids some stock? Is that a good way to lower the tax rate if it's increased in value significantly?

Giving kids some stock had always been a good way to lower the tax bill on the gains; because kids are generally in the lowest tax bracket, they'd pay capital gains taxes of just 5 percent on the profits (as long as the stocks were originally purchased more than a year ago), instead of the 15 percent capital gains rates that most parents pay. And the deal becomes even better from 2008 to 2010, when the long-term capital gains rate falls from 5 percent to 0 percent for people in the lowest two income-tax brackets.

But the tax law recently changed to add a twist to this strategy. In the past, your children's investment income would be taxed at your own rate until the kids turned 14, so you couldn't hide money in your kids' name just to avoid the tax bill (earned income, however, is taxed at your child's rate). And the law recently raised that age limit to 18. The first $850 of a child's investment earnings remains tax-free, and the next $850 is taxed at the child's rate in 2007, as it had been in the past. But any investment income beyond that $1,700 is now taxed in the parents' rate until the child turns 18, even if the investments are in a custodial account in the kid's name. You can still benefit from giving your child some stock, however, but you need to time it carefully. After age 18, the profits will be taxed at the kid's rate. And if your child turns 18 between 2008 and 2010, you could avoid the tax bill on the profits entirely.

The downside, however, is that 18 is the age of majority in some states (it's 21 in others). So at that age, the child takes control of money in a custodial account. If the kid still wants to spend it for college or another good cause, that's great. But if the kid wants to use the cash to buy a car, it's his money and he can legally make that purchase. Find out what the age limit is in your state and think carefully about what your kid is likely to do when he gets access to the account.

I own a business, and I've heard that I can get some good tax breaks if I hire my children to work in the office. How do those rules work?

It's true. If you own a business and have your children do legitimate work, you can write off their wages as a business expense, just like you would with other employees. It's a great way to lower your taxable income, and especially valuable because people who own their own business have to pay extra self-employment taxes on the money they earn. But the big benefit is that the children are in the lowest tax bracket and may not have to pay any income taxes on that money at all, if they earn less than $5,350 in 2007.

While this is a great way to lower your own taxable income, the work must be legitimate, such as copying documents, helping with mailings, making deliveries, or answering the phone. Your child's regular allowance doesn't count toward their earned wages. Every time your children work in your office, keep good records of when they worked, what they did, and how much you paid them. The pay also has to be reasonable for the job done. To maintain your records, it is best to pay your children with a check from your business account.

Tax Breaks for the Self-Employed

Last year, I started writing a monthly column for a local newspaper. I just received a 1099 from the newspaper reporting my income from them for the year (they hadn't withheld any taxes throughout the year). How do I report this on my taxes?

You'll report this self-employed income on Schedule C, "Profit or Loss From Business," when you file your taxes for the year, or you can report it on the simpler Schedule C-EZ if you had business expenses of $5,000 or less, had no employees, and aren't taking the home office deduction.

You'll also have to submit Schedule SE, on which you calculate your self-employment tax. That's the biggest downside to having self-employed income; when you're considered your own boss, you have to pay both the employee's and the employer's share of your Social Security and Medicare taxes on any freelance income, which adds an extra 7.65 percent to your tax rate.

The good news, though, is that more of your expenses are tax deductible. You'll be able to write off any business-related phone calls, mailings, equipment, travel, and maybe even the cost of a computer and printer you use for your freelance work. For more information, see IRS Publication 525, "Business Expenses." You might also be able to deduct your home office expenses—a portion of your rent or mortgage interest, homeowners' insurance, and utilities—if you use an area in your home exclusively for your business. For more information, see IRS Publication 587, "Business Use of Your Home." Also half of the self-employment taxes you pay are tax deductible.

When you have freelance income, you can also make tax-deductible contributions to a self-employed retirement plan, such as a SEP, an individual 401(k), a SIMPLE, or a Keogh. For more information about your options, see Chapter 1, Retirement Saving.

Because the newspaper isn't withholding any taxes from your paychecks, you should also file quarterly taxes in the future; otherwise, you could get hit with a penalty if you owe too much money when you file in April. You can either submit 1040-ES four times per year, or you or your spouse could increase your withholding from your other job to cover the extra income. See the small-business section at *www.irs.gov* for more information about paying estimated taxes, deducting business expenses, and the filing requirements for self-employed people.

If I start my own freelance business as a graphic designer, can I take advantage of the common business write-offs even if I keep my current full-time job with a corporation?

Y ou bet. In fact, you can deduct more than you earn in self-employment income for the year, as long as you are running a legitimate business.

As a graphic designer, you can deduct all sorts of business expenses on Schedule C, including the equipment you use primarily for freelance work, such as a new computer, fax machine, printer, separate phone line for business calls, and office furniture. You can also write off business-related travel, advertising, and printing costs. You can deduct a portion of your mortgage interest or rent, as well as utility bills, if a space in your home is used exclusively for your freelance job.

If business expenses exceed business income, subtract the extra costs from your other income. Taking a loss, however, might raise a red flag for the IRS, so be sure to document your expenses carefully to prove that your business is legitimate. If you lose money in three years out of five, the IRS generally considers your pursuit a hobby rather than a business, which makes it much more difficult for you to deduct expenses.

Use your profits to make tax-deductible contributions to a small-business retirement plan, such as an individual 401(k), which gives you the highest contribution limits even if you already have a 401(k) in your other job.

Deducting Charitable Contributions

What can I write off as a charitable contribution?

Y ou may be able to write off a lot more than you realize. Not only can you deduct money you give to an IRS-approved charity, but you can also deduct the current market value of goods you give, such as clothes and furniture. And you can give appreciated stock instead of cash, which could give you a bigger tax break, especially if the stock has increased significantly in value through the years (see page 179). But your charitable contributions are only tax deductible if you itemize.

Don't forget to check your pay stub for charitable contributions you may have automatically deducted from your paychecks, such as contributions to the United Way. And keep the receipts for your out-of-pocket expenses paid while helping a charity, such as volunteering at a school or helping with a charitable fundraiser.

You can also deduct parking fees, tolls, stamps, long-distance phone calls, and even the cost of ingredients you bought to cook for a homeless shelter. You'll also get a per-mile rate if you drove your car for charitable purposes (the rate is 14 cents per mile in 2007). Keep good records of all of your expenses.

What records do I need to provide to write off charitable contributions?

The rules just became a lot stricter. In the past, you could keep track of small contributions yourself, such as cash you place in a church collection basket. But now you can only deduct cash contributions if you can show a bank record or a written communication from the charity listing the amount of the contribution, the date it was made, and the name of the charity—even if the contribution is very small.

Because of the new rules, it's better to make all contributions by check rather than cash. If you no longer get your canceled checks mailed to you with your bank statements, it's a good idea to go through your bank records every month and print them out right away, so you don't end up having to pay the bank later to track down the receipts. And ask your church or other charity for documentation. Some churches keep a record of your weekly offering contributions and can give you a receipt at the end of the year, as long as you write your name on the offering envelope.

You don't need to send these records to the IRS when you file your taxes, but you do need to keep them in your files in case you're audited.

And if you contribute property that totals more than $5,000 in value in one year, you'll need to submit a written appraisal.

I plan to donate clothes to a charitable organization such as the Salvation Army. Where can I find the fair market value of the clothes—as well as household items I plan to donate—so I can write off my donation on my tax return? Is there a limit on how much I can deduct?

As you mentioned, you will only be able to deduct the fair market value of the clothes and other items that you give. That's the depreciated value of used goods, such as the price you'd pay in a thrift shop rather than the cost of buying them new.

Still, many people underestimate the amount they can deduct because they have no idea how to value the items. There are several tools, however, that can help.

The Salvation Army Web site (*www.salvationarmyusa .org*) has a useful valuation guide to help you figure out how much you can write off. It lists low and high values, and it's up to you to decide where your items fit based on their condition. Under a new tax law, you can only deduct items that are at least "good" condition, unless the item has been appraised at more than $500.

Another good tool is TurboTax's ItsDeductible software (*www.itsdeductible.com*), which gets its figures from research at resale stores and eBay data. It also automatically fills in IRS Form 8283 when your noncash donations exceed $500.

I'd like to make some charitable contributions before the end of the year so I can take the deduction on my taxes this year, but I haven't decided who to give the money to yet. Do you know of any good resources that can help me decide which charities to support?

Several Web sites make it easy to learn more about hundreds of charities and review their legitimacy and financial situations. The Better Business Bureau Wise Giving Alliance (*www.give.org*) and Charity Navigator (*www.charitynavigator.org*) have a lot of great information that can help you narrow your search.

Or you can buy yourself some time to do more research later. If you open up a donor-advised fund, you'll be able to donate the money now, get an income-tax deduction this year, and then invest the money while you have an unlimited amount of time to decide which charities to support. These funds are available at many mutual fund companies and brokerage firms, such as Charles Schwab, Fidelity, T. Rowe Price, and Vanguard. They generally require an initial contribution of $5,000 to $10,000. For lower contribution limits—and even more help with selecting which local charities to support—see if a community foundation in your area offers a donor-advised fund. Visit the community foundation locator on the Council of Foundations Web site (*www.cof.org/locator*) for links to local community foundations.

Donor-advised funds also make it easy to contribute stock in addition to cash, which can be complicated for some small charities to accept. Giving away stock or mutual fund shares can give you a bigger tax break if your investments have increased in value over the years. If you give appreciated stock, not only will you get to take a charitable deduction, but you'll also avoid paying capital gains taxes on the stock's gains. If you sold the stock and then donated the cash, on the other hand, you'd have to pay capital gains taxes first. It's also a good strategy if you've held the stock for a long time and are having trouble figuring out your cost basis. If you want to get rid of investments that have lost value, however, it's better to sell them first rather than give the shares to the charity. That way you can deduct your losses as well as deduct your charitable contribution.

Is it better to give a charity cash or appreciated stock?

I f the stock's price has risen significantly through the years, giving it to a charity is a great way to minimize your tax hit. You'll get a charitable deduction for the current value of the stock, and you'll avoid having to pay capital gains taxes on the stock's increase in value since you bought it. It's a great way to get out of paying taxes on stocks with huge gains, if you were going to give the money away anyway.

The difference in the tax bill can be big. If you sold the appreciated stock first and then gave cash to the charity, you'd have to pay the capital gains taxes first. Say, for example, you bought 100 shares of a stock for $500 and the value increased to $2,500 over the years. If you sold the stock first, you'd have to pay long-term capital gains taxes on the $2,000 in profits, most likely at the 15 percent rate. But if you gave the appreciated stock to a charity, you'd avoid the $300 capital gains tax bill. Meanwhile, you'll also be able to deduct the $2,500 gift as a charitable contribution, if you itemize.

On the other hand, if the stock you were going to donate had lost money, it's better to sell it first and then give the cash away. That way you can write off your capital loss and also get a charitable deduction for your contribution.

Tax Filing and Records

I just got married last December. Am I considered single or married for tax purposes? How should I file?

Your marital status on December 31st is your marital status for the whole year. The same is true for divorce. So even if you got married on New Year's Eve, Uncle Sam considers you to be married for the whole year.

You can either file jointly or married filing separately, although filing jointly is the best choice in almost all situations. If you're married filing separately, you'll give up access to a lot of important tax breaks; in most cases, you won't be eligible for a Roth IRA, for example, and can't take the Hope and lifetime learning credit for college costs.

One of the rare circumstances where filing separately can work, however, is if one of you has a lot of medical expenses and low income in one year. In that case, filing separately may make it a lot easier to pass the 7.5 percent adjusted gross income threshold for deducting medical expenses (you can only deduct medical expenses that weren't reimbursed by insurance or a health savings account or flexible-spending account after those costs exceed 7.5 percent of your adjusted gross income). Before you decide, though, run your numbers each way to see which option is best.

How long should it take to get my tax refund?

If your tax return and mailing address are accurate, you should receive your refund within six weeks after the IRS receives your return, which means that folks who filed by the April 15 deadline should get their checks by the end of May. If you filed electronically, you should receive your check within three weeks after the acknowledgment date; you'll get the money even faster if you have it deposited directly into your checking account. Refunds from amended returns are usually issued within 8 to 12 weeks.

It's easy to check on the status of your refund. Go to the IRS's Refund Status tool at *www.irs.gov* and type in your Social Security number, filing status, and the exact dollar amount of the refund you're expecting. You'll immediately find out whether your return was received by the IRS and is in processing, if the refund check has already been mailed, or if a refund has been returned to the IRS because it couldn't be delivered to your address. If you have additional questions, call the IRS's refund hotline at 800-829-1954.

One of the most common reasons for a delay is that the IRS doesn't have your current address. For more information about updating your address, see IRS Tax Topic 157, "How to Notify the IRS of a Change of Address," at *www.irs.gov*. Filing errors can also cause a delay, such as if you forgot to sign the return or include your Social Security number.

I'm self-employed and I was just going through my office and discovered some old receipts from business expenses I forgot to deduct when I filed my taxes last year. Can I deduct these expenses on next year's taxes so I can finally get credit for them?

If you spent the money last year, you'll need to deduct the expenses on your taxes for that year; you can't just add them on to next year's return. But it isn't too late to make a change to last year's taxes and possibly get an extra refund.

You have up to three years after the original due date of your return to file an amended return if you've made a mistake or left something out. To make the change, print out Form 1040-X and fill in the numbers from your original return and then the changes you're making. You'll also need to submit a new Schedule C, "Profit or Loss From Business," because you're adding additional business expenses. Also contact your state's department of revenue about amending your state income-tax return.

Before you make the change, keep in mind that it could affect other areas of your finances. Adding more business expenses, for example, will lower your self-employed income and may decrease the amount of money you could have contributed to a small-business retirement account for that year. If you'd need to take back some of the contributions, adding the extra business expenses may not be worth the hassle (and may not save you quite as much money as you'd originally expect, because you're giving up some tax-deductible contributions). Calculate the tax savings yourself before deciding to submit the amended return.

I've finally decided to get rid of a lot of old papers and keep myself more organized. With that in mind, I'm wondering, what financial records do I need to keep and what can I throw away?

It's great to weed out and organize your financial records at least once a year—especially near New Year's. As soon as you receive some of your year-end statements, you can toss a lot of the papers that are filling up your file cabinets. And it's a great time to get a head start on gathering your tax paperwork, instead of scrambling to find everything at the last minute and missing out on valuable deductions. Here's what you can get rid of and what you'll need to track down:

- *Bank records.* Toss ATM receipts after your bank statement arrives and you've made sure everything matches up. You probably aren't receiving your canceled checks anymore, but you may get images of the checks with your statements or can download them from the bank's Web site. Now is a good time to print out and keep copies that you may need for tax purposes, for example, to document charitable contributions or business expenses. If you paid the bills online, your bank statement showing to whom the money was transferred can count for tax purposes.

- *Tax records.* It's a good idea to keep your returns forever, but you can generally toss your supporting documents three years after you filed your taxes; you're usually safe from being audited after that time unless you forgot to report a big chunk of your income. If you have any self-employment income, keep the records for at least six years.

- *Investments.* Keep records showing what you originally paid for mutual funds and stocks until you sell them and report the gain or loss on your taxes. Also hold on to your year-end statements showing how much you received in dividends or capital gains distributions during the year, so you won't end up paying taxes on them twice if you reinvest that money. You can toss your monthly statements if everything matches up with your year-end report.
- *Home-improvement records.* Because most homeowners can keep their home sale profits tax free, they don't generally think to keep home-improvement records anymore. But it's still useful to hold on to the receipts because you could end up paying a tax bill when you sell your home if you have lived in it for less than two years, if you end up renting out part of it, or if you end up with more than $250,000 in profit if single, $500,000 if married. All home improvements that add value to your home (not just regular repairs) can lower your tax bill. The information can also help document the work you've put into the house when you go to sell it.
- *Credit card statements.* Throw them away as soon as your payment is posted on the next month's bill, unless you need to keep them for your tax records.
- *Utility receipts.* Toss them as soon as the next month's statement shows that you paid the bill, unless you're deducting them as a home office expense.

I received a $1,000 refund from my taxes last year, and although it felt good to get that much cash, I could have really used it in my paychecks during the year. What do I need to do so I can increase my paychecks now instead?

You have the right idea. Getting a big fat tax refund might feel good at the time, but most people really could have used the extra money in their paychecks. Instead of giving the IRS essentially a tax-free loan for the year, adjust your withholding so you can benefit from that extra money now. It's a good idea for anyone who received more than a $500 refund or owed more than 10 percent of their total tax bill to adjust withholding. For most taxpayers, it's based on the number of allowances claimed on the W-4. That's the form on file with your employer that helps determine the amount of tax withheld from your paychecks.

Most people fill out that form when they first take a job and don't ever see or think about it again. However, you can change the number of allowances at any time. The more allowances you claim, the less is withheld. Some taxpayers, especially two-income couples, may find that they're underwithholding even though they're claiming zero allowances. The IRS solves this problem with a line on the W-4 that lets you tell your employer how much more to take out of your paycheck.

Anything that lowers your tax bill—exemptions, tax credits, deductions, and losses—can be considered in your allowance calculation. Did you get married, divorced, or have a child? Did you purchase a new home, refinance, or take out a home equity loan? Did your portfolio tank, leaving you with big capital losses? Did you get a raise or earn less this year than last?

The easiest way to check your withholding is by using the IRS Withholding Calculator at *www.irs.gov*. This step-by-step wizard walks you through the calculation. You simply answer a few questions and plug in the withholding amounts from your most recent pay stubs and your most recent tax return. The calculator estimates your tax bill, how far over or under that figure your withholding will be, and recommends how many allowances you should claim. The calculator does not account for investment losses, however. If you have $3,000 or more of net losses, you can claim an extra withholding allowance.

If you prefer to evaluate your W-4 the old fashioned way, download IRS Publication 919, "How Do I Adjust My Tax Withholding?" It contains all the worksheets and instructions you will need to work through the calculations on your own. For a much faster estimate, see the withholding calculator at Kiplinger.com.

Once you calculate your allowances, download a new W-4 from IRS.gov, fill it out, and turn it in to your human resources office.

Tax Breaks from a Flexible Spending Account

Help! It's almost the end of the year and I still have about $1,000 left in my health care flexible spending account. I totally misjudged my medical expenses for the year. What can I do? I don't want to lose the money.

First of all, you may not need to worry. Some companies now give employees up until mid-March to use up the money in their flexible spending accounts.

And even if your employer doesn't offer the extra time, there are a few things you can do to use up the money quickly. You can use the health care flexible spending account money on your health insurance deductibles, co-payments, dental work, orthodontia, out-of-pocket expenses for fertility treatments, and other medical expenses that aren't covered by insurance. That might be tough to do suddenly in the last few weeks of the year.

There also are a few last-minute things you can do to use up the money. You can spend the FSA money on prescription and certain nonprescription drugs, so a trip to the drug store to stock up on aspirin and cold medicine could use up a chunk of your cash (you can't use the money, however, on vitamins). If you take prescription medications, see if you can order the next few months' supply in advance. You can also use the money for eyeglasses, contact lenses, and prescription sunglasses, which you can probably do on short notice. Doctor-recommended weight-loss programs and a trip to the chiropractor can count too. Even a last-minute appointment with the dentist can help you clean out your account.

If you don't use up all of the money in your account, you can still come out ahead because of the tax breaks. If you set aside $3,000 in your flex account and you usually pay about 33 percent of your income in federal, state, and Social Security taxes, for example, you only have to spend about $2,000 to break even.

I heard that if you claim a reimbursement from your flex account, it should be paid even if there is not currently enough in your account, as long as there will eventually be enough money to cover the claim based on future contributions for the year. Is that correct?

Yes, that's right. You can use the full year's amount of flex plan money at the beginning of the year, even though you'll be making contributions throughout the year. Even if you spend the whole amount and then leave your job after the first few months, you generally don't have to pay back the money. This is one reason why many employers cap flexible spending account contributions at $2,000 to 3,000 for the year.

On the flip side, though, you can't change your contribution level in the middle of the year unless you have a change in family status, such as if you get married, have a child, or get divorced. And you'll lose any money in the account that you haven't spent by the end of the year (some employers extend the deadline until mid-March of the next year). That's good to keep in mind toward the end of year, when you only have a couple months to clean out the account. You can use the money for almost any health-related expenses that aren't covered by insurance, including deductibles, co-payments, dental work, orthodontia, prescription sunglasses, eyeglasses, contact lenses, out-of-pocket expenses for fertility treatments, chiropractic care, doctor-recommended weight-loss programs, and prescription and over-the-counter medications, as well as many other costs.

As you're planning for next year's flexible spending account, keep in mind that many health plans are increasing their co-payments, deductibles, and out-of-pocket costs for medical care and prescription drugs—all of which can be paid with pretax money from your flexible spending account. And you don't even have to spend the whole amount of money in the account to come out ahead. If you set aside $3,000 in your flex plan and usually pay 33 percent in federal, state, and Social Security taxes, you only have to spend about $2,000 to break even. To run your own numbers, see the flexible spending account calculator in the Tools section of Kiplinger.com.

What happens to the $1,000 I already put in my flexible spending account for this year? I got laid off with one day's notice and had no medical bills yet for which to get reimbursed. Does my company have the right to keep the flex plan money or should this $1,000 be reimbursed to me?

You normally lose any flex plan money that you haven't used when you leave your job. But there is a way to buy some extra time to access the money—if you know how to ask.

First, see if your employer will give you until the end of the month to use the money, which is an option under some employer's plans.

Or you may be able to get more time by signing up for COBRA benefits, the same federal law that lets employees keep group health insurance for up to 18 months after they leave their jobs. Most companies with 20 or more employees must offer COBRA coverage, which also applies to flexible spending account money (you don't have to elect COBRA for health insurance in order to have a COBRA flex plan).

To keep your FSA open, you'd continue making your same monthly contribution plus a 2 percent charge; so if you'd signed up to contribute $1,200 for the year to your FSA and had $100 per month deducted from your paycheck, you'd pay $102 per month and still have access to your FSA.

Then you can pay for COBRA for just a month or two while you get back your money. You'll be able to use the $100 of the monthly COBRA charges, as well as the $1,000 you already contributed, for medical expenses.

You can use FSA money for eyeglasses, contact lenses, prescription and many nonprescription medications, dental care, chiropractor visits, deductibles and co-pays, and many other medical expenses that aren't covered by insurance.

Financial Strategies After You've Retired

After spending decades saving for retirement, many people aren't prepared for the total change in financial strategy after they stop working. You're no longer worried about accumulating the biggest nest egg, but you now need to know how to stretch the money as far as possible so you don't outlive your income. If you spend too much in the early years, you could end up struggling financially at the end of your life, even if you started with substantial savings. And there are far fewer opportunities to catch up after the money is gone.

That's why making the most of the financial rules in retirement can make a big difference, and why I receive so many questions from retirees. Understanding the tax laws and Social Security choices becomes even more important when every dollar you save can help preserve more money in your retirement fund. And figuring out how to deal with one of the biggest retiree expenses—health care—can have a giant impact on your cash flow. Even after you qualify for Medicare, the government program still leaves many gaps, and many options for filling them. And the new Medicare prescription drug program changes all of your options. The strategies that worked just a few years ago may no longer be your best solution.

Here's how to make the most of your financial choices so you can afford to live a full life in retirement.

How to Guarantee Lifetime Income

How can I avoid running out of money in retirement?

That's the most complicated question for retirement savers because you have no idea how long the money needs to last. Using average life expectancy numbers doesn't help because half the people live longer than that, and if you do, you could have very little money to live on for the last several years of your life. To get an idea of your life expectancy based on your habits and history, go to Northwestern Mutual's Longevity Game Web site (*www.longevitygame.com*). Regardless of the answer you find there, though, it's better to use big numbers in your calculations—such as age 100 or higher—just to be safe.

If your life expectancy is around 30 years, there's a simple calculation that can help you stretch your retirement savings and make it unlikely that you'll outlive your money: start by withdrawing just 4 percent of your personal savings during your first year in retirement and adjust future withdrawals to compensate for inflation. That's a conservative rule of thumb, but it would protect you even if you happen to retire during a bear market and end up having to withdraw funds from a dwindling balance. That means if you have $1 million in savings, you'd start by withdrawing $40,000.

It's also a good idea to run your numbers through T. Rowe Price's retirement income calculator (*www.troweprice.com/ric*), which lets you know when you're likely to run out of money if you continue spending at your current pace. The calculator is particularly helpful because it uses Monte Carlo simulations, running your numbers through hundreds of potential investment scenarios to figure the probability that your money will last for a certain time period, no matter what happens to the stock market during that time. This is important because the future of your nest egg varies enormously depending on the performance of your investments and interest rates when you start withdrawing the money—regardless of what ends up happening with the average returns. A few tough years at the beginning of your retirement can make a huge difference in how long your nest egg can last.

It's also a good idea to run your numbers through the calculator again every few years to make sure you're still on track. If it looks like you'll fall short, you could stretch your money by lowering your monthly withdrawals or investing more aggressively. If you're 65 years old, for example, your portfolio is likely to last much longer if you keep 65 percent in stocks rather than 15 percent in stocks, because your money has greater opportunity for growth over the long run. Or you could always work for a few more years, which can do wonders for your retirement savings. Because you won't need to tap the money as quickly, you may even be able to keep saving, and you'll need the money for fewer years after you finally do retire. See Chapter 1, Retirement Saving, for more information.

Another way to guarantee that you'll continue to have some income for life is to invest some of your money in an immediate annuity, which promises to provide regular income for as long as you (or you and a beneficiary) live—even if it's much longer than your life expectancy. See the next page for more information about selecting an annuity and deciding how much money to invest.

I am fast approaching retirement age and am looking for answers on how to best use my 401(k), which is the only plan that I have. I have been told to roll it into an immediate annuity, which I know nothing about. Is this a good idea?

Having some money in an immediate annuity can be a good way to make sure you don't outlive your income in retirement. Immediate annuities are very different from deferred annuities, which people use as a tax-deferred way to save for retirement. In many cases, deferred annuities aren't a good deal because of the fees, especially if the money is already in a 401(k).

With an immediate annuity, on the other hand, you invest a lump of money after retirement and start to receive payouts immediately. The checks can continue for the rest of your life, or as long as you and your spouse live, or for a certain number of years (10 years is common), even if you both die before then. This can be a great way to guarantee you'll have some money coming in for the rest of your life, especially if you don't have a pension. And it's a good way to maximize your payouts; you'll be able to tap your principal as well as income because you know that payouts are guaranteed for life.

But it's a bad idea to invest all of your money in an immediate annuity. It's generally tough to access the principal after you've given it to the insurance company, which can make life difficult if you have an emergency or need more than your regular monthly check (some companies allow access to the money, but you'll usually pay extra for that flexibility). And in order to receive the highest payouts, your heirs won't receive anything after you—or you and your spouse—die.

Instead of investing all of your 401(k) money in an immediate annuity, it's better just to invest a piece of your retirement funds there. To calculate the amount, work backwards; start by figuring out your monthly expenses in retirement, and then subtract any sources of guaranteed income you already have to cover them, such as Social Security or a pension, and invest enough money in an immediate annuity to provide a monthly income that can fill in any gap.

It's generally best to invest 30 percent or less of your retirement income in the annuity, so the rest is still accessible. After you know you have enough guaranteed income to pay your monthly bills, you can generally invest the rest of your retirement money more aggressively, which could eventually result in more money to leave to your heirs, keep up with inflation, or use for other expenses.

To calculate how much money you'll need to invest to provide that amount of monthly income, run your numbers through the calculator at ImmediateAnnuities .com. It's generally best to go with the company that offers the highest monthly payout—as long as it's a solid company—rather than focus too much on the company's advertised interest rate. A company that touts a high interest rate could actually have a lower monthly payout because of high fees.

I'm 75 and have been retired for several years. I'm worried that I might outlive my retirement savings and I would like to spend some of my money to buy an immediate annuity that guarantees a payout for life. If I invest $100,000, how much monthly income can I get?

If you buy a fixed immediate annuity, your payout will remain the same for life. But the specific payout amount varies depending on the interest rates when you buy the annuity. In November 2006, a 75-year-old man who invested $100,000 in an immediate annuity could receive as much as $938 per month for the rest of his life ($11,256 per year), according to ImmediateAnnuities .com. The payout amounts are based on the interest rates at the time you invest in the immediate annuity.

If he submitted medical records showing he had a health condition that could lower his life expectancy— such as heart disease, most cancers, or diabetes—some companies may offer him even more money each month, as if he bought the annuity at an older age. Vanguard, AIG, Genworth, and Lincoln Benefit Life are a few of the companies currently offering these medically underwritten annuities. Most other companies give you the same payout as everyone else your age, regardless of your medical condition.

The payout amount shrinks if you'd like the checks to continue even after you die. The monthly payout would be $727 (or $8,724 per year) if you wanted to receive the checks as long as you or your 75-year-old spouse lives. And you'd only get $667 per month if you'd like payouts to continue for as long as you or your spouse lives or at least ten years, if you both die before then.

Some companies also let you buy an annuity that increases its payout amount every year for inflation or lets you access some of the principal in an emergency, both in return for a lower payout to start.

I received information from the American Cancer Society about buying a charitable gift annuity, which could benefit the organization and give me income. Is this a good idea?

I t depends on your goals. A charitable gift annuity won't give you the highest payout, but it will help you support a charity, receive a lifetime income, and get some big tax breaks too. It's a way to give money to a charity now rather than waiting until after you die, without having to worry about giving too much and running out of income.

Most charities, including the American Cancer Society, use standard rates set by the American Council on Gift Annuities, which is currently paying 6 percent for life if you invest the money at age 65, 6.5 percent if you buy at age 70, 7.1 percent if you buy at age 75, 8.0 percent at age 80, and 11.3 percent at age 90 and above (see *www.acga-web.org/giftrates.html* for the full list). A 65-year-old who contributes $100,000 to a gift annuity, for example, will immediately start receiving $6,000 per year for life. The payouts represent a return of principal as well as interest, so only part is taxable.

The payouts are lower if you choose a joint annuity, which pays out as long as you or your spouse is alive. For example, if a 65-year-old man and his 70-year-old wife contribute $100,000 to an American Cancer Society charitable gift annuity, they'd receive $5,700 per year as long as either one lives. If the couple bought a regular immediate annuity from an insurance company, on the other hand, they could get as much as $7,320 per year as long as either one lives, according to ImmediateAnnuities.com.

About half the money you invest in the charitable gift annuity ends up supporting the charity, and you do get several tax breaks you wouldn't get with a commercial annuity. The 65- and 70-year-old couple would get a tax deduction of $32,381 for their charitable contribution, which could save them $8,095 in taxes in the 25 percent bracket.

You can get an extra tax break if you donate appreciated stock, which can lower the capital gains tax bill that you'd owe if you sold the stock yourself. By giving the money now rather than after you die, you keep the money out of your estate and the charity has more years to benefit from the funds.

Because a charitable gift annuity is a long-term contract that may pay out for decades, it's best to work with an established charity that should be around for a while. Check out the charity at the Better Business Bureau's Wise Giving Alliance (*www.give.org*) or Charity Navigator (*www.charitynavigator.org*). Then contact the charity's development office, which can show you the payout amounts and tax breaks for your specific situation and walk you through the process.

IRA and 401(k) Withdrawal Rules

I turned 70½ last year and took my first IRA required minimum distribution this April. A friend of mine told me that I'd have to take another distribution by the end of the year. Is this true? Why is that the case?

Your friend is right. You don't need to take your first IRA distribution until April 1 of the year after the year you turn 70½. That's considered your distribution for age 70. But you'll also have to take your distribution for age 71 in that year, too, which you must do by December 31. After that first year, you must make all required minimum distributions by December 31. If you don't withdraw the right amount of money, you'll have to pay a 50 percent penalty on the amount of money you should have withdrawn but didn't.

To calculate how much money you need to withdraw, take the balance of your IRA accounts as of December 31 of the previous year and divide it by the number you'll find in the IRS tables for someone your age. You can use the tables at the end of IRS Publication 590 (available at *www.irs.gov*) or the calculator in the Retirement Tools section of Kiplinger.com. These calculations are based on your life expectancy. You'll need to use a different table if your beneficiary is a spouse who is more than ten years younger than you.

Do the same thing by December 31 the following year, based on the previous year's account balance and the IRS divisor based on your new age.

These rules only apply to traditional IRAs. You don't need to make any required minimum distributions from Roth IRAs.

I have several IRAs. Can I satisfy the minimum distribution requirement from only one IRA instead of taking the money from each one?

Yes. Even though you'll need to calculate the required minimum distribution from each IRA, and then add them all up, you can take the money from whichever one you want.

Withdrawals are fully taxable if all of your money is in tax-deductible IRAs. If some of your money is in nondeductible IRAs, then a portion of your withdrawals will be a tax-free return of principal, while the earnings (and tax-deductible contributions) will be taxable.

Is there any way I can avoid the 50 percent penalty if I don't take my required IRA distributions after age 70½?

The IRS may waive the penalty if you have a good excuse, such as if illness prevented you from making the required withdrawal or if you relied on bad advice about how much you were required to withdraw. Otherwise, once you reach age 70½, you have to withdraw a minimum amount from a traditional IRA each year. The amount is based on your life expectancy and is designed to get all the money out of the account—with tax paid—by the time you die. See the tables in IRS Publication 590 for the specific calculations.

Also there is now another way to avoid paying taxes on your IRA withdrawals. You'll still need to make your required minimum distributions by the deadline (April 1 of the year after the year you turn 70½, December 31 after that), but a new tax law now lets you donate up to $100,000 per year from your IRA tax free to a charity in 2006 and 2007. To qualify, you must be at least 70½ when you make the contribution. The donation satisfies the rules for required minimum distributions, and donated amounts won't be taxed or included in your adjusted gross income. If you were planning to contribute money to a charity anyway, this is a great way to avoid the income-tax bill on gains in your IRA, which are taxed at your income-tax rate. You can't double dip deductions, though; you won't be able to take a charitable deduction for any portion of these withdrawals that would have been taxable otherwise. (See additional details on the next page.)

I understand that a new tax law lets people who are 70½ or older send their required minimum distribution from their IRA to a charity and not pay taxes on it. I have two questions: Can you also use this charitable contribution as a deduction if you itemize deductions? And are you required to transfer the gift directly to the charity or can you withdraw it and send the check to the charity?

The Pension Protection Act of 2006 changed several laws related to pensions and retirement savings. But it also included some new charitable-giving rules. The biggest news for retirees is the change in the law permitting charitable donations of IRA money. For 2006 and 2007, people age 70½ and older can give up to $100,000 per year from their IRA directly to a charity and avoid paying income taxes on the money (even if it's a lot more than your required minimum distribution).

These new rules are particularly helpful for retirees who need to take required minimum distributions from traditional IRAs that have increased significantly in value through the years—and would owe a big income-tax bill on their withdrawals—but don't need the money on which to live. The contribution counts as your required distribution but isn't included in your adjusted gross income.

If you avoid the tax bill when you give away your IRA money, however, you can't write off the charitable contribution too. But you don't have to itemize to qualify, which finally gives retirees some tax benefits for charitable gifts even after they've paid off their homes and are taking the standard deduction.

The money must be transferred directly from the IRA trustee to the charity (contributions to donor-advised funds aren't eligible), which could cause some logistical complications. Talk with the IRA trustee and the charity first about what documentation you need to provide to make sure the charity knows who gave the gift and can give you a receipt for your tax records. The American Red Cross, for example, offers a letter of instruction that donors can give to their IRA trustee and the charity, which makes it easy for everyone to know whom the money is coming from and where it's going.

Making the Most of Social Security

When can I start to receive full retirement benefits from Social Security?

It depends on when you were born. For years, the age for full retirement benefits was 65. But as life expectancy started to increase—and Social Security struggled to pay many more years of benefits—the government increased the age for full benefits. It's still 65 for people who were born in 1937 or earlier, but it's now 65 and two months if you're born in 1938, 65 and four months if you're born in 1939, and gradually increases by two months every year until 1943. Full retirement age is 66 for people born in 1943 to 1954. Then it gradually increases by two months for every year until it hits age 67 for people born in 1960 or later.

What happens if I don't take Social Security at my full retirement age? When should I take the benefits?

You can start taking Social Security either a few years before or after full retirement age, although it will affect your payout amount.

You can take Social Security benefits as early as age 62, but your checks will be reduced by up to 25 percent for the rest of your life (for the specific reduction, see the table at *www.ssa.gov/retirechartred.htm*).

Your benefits will be reduced even further if you take Social Security early and continue to work. If you earn more than $12,960 in 2007 and take Social Security before your full retirement age, you'll forfeit $1 in benefits for every $2 you make over the limit, which makes it a horrible idea to take early Social Security benefits if you still work. That earnings cap disappears once you reach your full retirement age.

If you aren't working, however, you could take the benefits at age 62 and invest them. You can save money because you won't have to tap your tax-deferred retirement funds quite as early, which lets you delay the tax bill even longer.

But taking early benefits isn't as good a deal for married couples. A surviving spouse is entitled to 100 percent of the primary wage earner's benefits. So if you want to leave the most income for your spouse, it's best to wait until normal retirement age or later to tap Social Security benefits.

And if you live a long time, you may benefit by waiting even longer. If you reach your normal retirement age in 2008 or later, your benefits increase by 8 percent every year that you delay benefits until age 70. You have to live for several years after that in order to make up for the years you went without benefits, but if you live for a long time, waiting can give you more money. You can run your numbers and find your break-even point with the Social Security Administration's online benefits calculators (*www.ssa.gov/planners/calculators.htm*).

I'm a military retiree and am thinking of taking Social Security at age 62. Will my military pension count against the $12,960 I can earn before losing Social Security benefits?

No. The Social Security earnings test counts only wages and self-employment income. Investment earnings, pension payments, and IRA withdrawals don't count.

I'm 55 and have worked full time since I was 21. If I drop to part-time status, and cut my salary to 80 percent of my current $53,000, will that affect my Social Security benefits at age 66?

Benefits are based on your 35 highest earning years. If you retire before working for that long, the calculation includes a $0 for each missing year. Because you've already worked for 34 years, staying full-time for one extra year could make a difference—especially if your salary was much lower (after adjusting for inflation) for many of the years.

To see how much of a difference it can make, dig up a copy of your Social Security earnings statement, which lists how much you've paid into the system since you started working. You should have received a statement around your birthday. Then run your numbers through the benefits calculator at the Social Security Web site (*www.socialsecurity.gov*) to see what your payouts would be under several scenarios. You can also order an earnings statement at the Social Security Web site if you can't find your copy.

Will my Social Security income be taxed?

It depends on how much money you earn. Taxes on Social Security benefits are based on your "provisional income," which is basically your income from a job and taxable investments plus any tax-free municipal bond income and 50 percent of your Social Security benefits.

If you're single and your provisional income is less than $25,000, or less than $32,000 if you file a joint return, then your benefits are tax free. If the total is more than that, then part of your benefits will be taxed. If you're single and your provisional income is between

$25,000 and $34,000 (or $32,000 to $44,000 if married filing jointly), then 50 percent of your Social Security benefits are taxable. If you're single with a provisional income of more than $34,000 (or $44,000 if married), then 85 percent of your Social Security benefits are taxable.

You should receive a report from the Social Security Administration every year (SSA-1099) showing how much money you received in benefits. Use those numbers when you fill out the worksheet in your tax instructions to make sure you pay the right amount.

Dealing with Medicare and Health Insurance

I'm retiring early (age 60) and my biggest expense will be medical insurance. How can I reduce this cost?

You won't be eligible for Medicare until age 65, but you have several other options until then. First, see if you're eligible for any retiree health insurance from your former employer. If coverage is available, that's usually your best bet. If not, you can still continue coverage for up to 18 months after you leave your job through COBRA, a federal law that requires employers with 20 or more employees to let you stay on the employer plan for a limited time after you leave the group. This coverage, however, can be very expensive. Many employers generally cover 75 percent or more of their employees' premiums, but when you're on COBRA, you have to foot 100 percent of the bill yourself—plus up to 2 percent in administrative charges.

If you have any medical problems, COBRA can be your best bet because insurers can't reject you or charge a higher rate because of your health condition. But otherwise you might find a better deal on your own.

As long as you're relatively healthy and live in a state with a competitive health insurance marketplace (most states other than New York or New Jersey, for example), an individual health insurance policy may cost a lot less than you'd expect. The average premium is $4,185 per year for people age 60 to 64 buying single coverage and $7,248 for family coverage, according to America's Health Insurance Plans, a trade group for health insurers.

And you can cut your costs even further by buying a high-deductible health insurance policy and opening up a health savings account. Almost anyone under age 65 who buys a qualified health insurance policy with a deductible of at least $1,100 for individual coverage, $2,200 for families in 2007, can open an HSA, which lets you set aside pretax money up to an annual maximum of $2,850 for individuals, $5,650 for families in 2007, plus an extra $800 if you're 55 or older. You can use the money tax free for medical expenses, and anything left over grows tax deferred. You can use the money for anything after age 65 without penalty, but you will owe income taxes on any money that isn't used for medical expenses.

In many cases, the cost savings from buying a high-deductible policy more than make up for the higher out-of-pocket medical expenses you may have to pay, especially considering that most people usually don't spend their full deductible. And the tax benefits give it an added boost. It's one of the only ways you can set aside pretax money that grows tax deferred and is available tax free, regardless of your income level. And unlike a flexible spending account at work, which also lets you set aside pretax money for medical expenses, you don't need to use the HSA money by the end of the year. Instead, it can accumulate for future medical expenses that you can use whether you're younger or older than age 65 (you generally can't continue to contribute to an HSA, however, after age 65).

You can use the money for all kinds of medical expenses that aren't covered by your insurance policy, including your deductible, co-payments, and other out-of-pocket costs. And there are plenty of things to spend it on even after you turn 65 and qualify for Medicare, including your Medicare premiums and co-pays for Parts A, B, C, or D (the prescription drug plan). You can also use the money to pay for qualified long-term care insurance. But you can't use it to pay Medigap premiums.

For more information about health savings accounts, see Chapter 3, Save Money on Insurance.

I realize that the age for full Social Security retirement benefits is no longer 65. Has the age also changed for Medicare?

The age for Medicare eligibility hasn't changed; you can still receive benefits at age 65, even if you start taking Social Security benefits after that. But you bring up an excellent point that can lead to a lot of confusion. People born in 1938 won't actually qualify for full Social Security benefits until they're 65 and two months. People born in 1939 can't get full benefits until they reach 65 and four months; it's 65 and six months for people born in 1940, and the Social Security eligibility age gradually rises until it reaches age 67 for people born in 1960 or later. (See above for more details.)

But the age for Medicare eligibility isn't increasing; it remains age 65. In the past, most people receiving Social Security benefits were automatically enrolled in Medicare when they turned age 65. But now, if you wait until you sign up for Social Security to enroll in Medicare, you will miss a few months of coverage *and* you could get stuck with a penalty.

The initial enrollment period for Medicare is from three months before to three months after your 65th birthday. So if you don't sign up for Medicare before you qualify for full Social Security benefits, you may have to wait until the next general enrollment period to sign up—from January to March each year—and your coverage won't start until the following July. Plus, you could get hit with a permanent premium penalty of 10 percent for every 12-month period you delay enrollment, as long as you don't have other primary coverage (through an employer, for example).

Instead of waiting, you'll need to sign up for Medicare during your initial enrollment period, no matter when you become eligible for full Social Security benefits. Call 800-772-1213 to find the nearest Social Security office. Also check out Medicare.gov's Medicare Eligibility Tool and the Social Security Administration's Web site (*www.socialsecurity.gov*) for more information about signing up for Medicare.

Hopefully you can help. My husband will turn 65 in a few months, so we're starting to think about his health care coverage. Do we need to get a Medigap policy or will Medicare cover most everything?

Even though Medicare will cover a lot of his medical bills after he turns 65, it still leaves some big gaps, including substantial deductibles, co-payments for doctor and hospital visits, and no automatic coverage for prescription drugs. If you're lucky enough to have retiree health insurance through your employer, it's usually your best choice. But most people no longer have that option.

In that case, it's a good idea to buy a Medicare supplement policy (also called Medigap) and stand-alone Medicare Part D prescription drug coverage, or have both your medical and prescription coverage together in a Medicare Advantage plan, which generally includes Medicare HMOs, regional preferred-provider organizations (PPOs), which can span several states, and also a few new private fee-for-service plans that let you use any doctor.

If you'd like to buy a Medigap plan, first pick which type of coverage you'd like to get. The government lets insurers offer several standardized plans: A through G, as well as new plans K and L in 2006. (Insurers can no longer sell plans H, I, and J to new customers, which provided limited prescription drug coverage but weren't subsidized by the government and tended to be a lot more expensive than the new Medicare prescription drug plan.)

Medigap plan A covers the $248 daily co-payment for days 61 to 90 in a hospital in 2007, the $496 co-payment for days 91 to 150, and payment in full for 365 additional hospital days during your lifetime, as well as the 20 percent co-payment for doctor's services and the cost of three pints of blood. All Medigap plans cover these basic benefits and, as you move through the alphabet, coverage expands and premiums generally rise. Plan F is the most popular. The new plans K and L cover 50 percent and 75 percent of the in-patient hospital deductible and the co-payment for doctors' services (most of the other plans cover 100 percent of those expenses), in return for a lower deductible. You can generally use any doctor anywhere, which is particularly helpful if you have a specialist you want to work with or travel frequently.

See the Medicare plans and benefits table at the Medicare Rights Center Web site for a listing of each plan's features *(www.medicarerights.org/medigap_options. html)* Most state insurance departments list prices for Medigap plans available in your area (find your state's site at *www.naic.org*). If you buy a Medigap policy, you should generally buy a separate Medicare Part D plan for your prescription drug coverage too. To shop for a plan, input information about your prescriptions into Medicare.gov's prescription drug plan finder (*www .medicare.gov/mpdpf*), which shows your premiums plus out-of-pocket costs for the drugs you take through the plans available in your area.

Instead of signing up for Medicare plus a Medigap plan and Part D policy, you could get all of your health insurance in one policy through a Medicare Advantage plan. These policies used to be just Medicare HMOs, which limited your coverage to certain doctors and hospitals and weren't a good idea if you traveled frequently or owned a vacation home in another part of the country. But they've recently expanded to include regional preferred provider organizations, and even offer some plans—called private fee-for-service—that let you use any doctor anywhere. These policies generally provide coverage for doctors, hospitals, and prescription drugs. The premiums tend to be lower than the cost of Medicare plus a Medigap plan and stand-alone Part D coverage, but you may have more out-of-pocket expenses.

You can get price quotes and coverage details for Medigap or Medicare Advantage plans in your area by using Medicare.gov's Medicare options compare tool (*www.medicare.gov/mppf*).

What's this I hear about Medicare premiums now being based on your income? Will this change my monthly cost by a lot?

For the first time ever, the 2007 premiums for Medicare Part B will be based on your income.

The monthly cost won't change significantly for most people. Couples earning $160,000 or less (based on your 2005 adjusted gross income plus tax-exempt interest income) and single filers earning $80,000 or less will pay $93.50 per person per month for Medicare Part B, which covers physician services and outpatient hospital visits. That's just a 5.6 percent increase over last year's cost.

But if you earn more than those levels, you'll pay from $106 to $162 per month. Individuals earning more than $200,000 and couples earning more than $400,000 will pay the top price, which is nearly double the $88.50 monthly premium for 2006.

MEDICARE PART B PREMIUMS FOR 2007

Single Filer Income	Joint Filer Income	Monthly Part B Premium
$80,000 or less	$160,000 or less	$93.50
$80,001 to $100,000	$160,001 to $200,000	$106.00
$100,001 to $150,000	$200,001 to $300,000	$124.70
$150,001 to $200,000	$300,001 to $400,000	$143.40
More than $200,000	More than $400,000	$162.10

If your income has dropped since 2005 because you retired or your spouse died, or you experienced certain other life-changing events, then you can ask the Social Security Administration to re-calculate your premiums, which may reduce the cost. Call the Social Security Administration at 800-772-1213 or visit a local field office for more information.

My mother is paying $171 per month for her
Medicare supplement insurance policy. Is that
about right? How do I shop for a Medigap policy?

That sounds in the ballpark, but the specifics vary a lot depending on her age, where she lives, and the type of policy she has. The average cost for the most popular Medigap policy, called plan F, is $1,813 per year for a 65-year-old woman, according to Weiss Ratings— just a little less than the $2,052 per year that your mom is paying now. Older policyholders with richer policies generally pay more.

But it's still a great time for your mom to check out her options. The new Medicare prescription drug plan introduced some interesting alternatives while making some of the old Medigap policies horrible deals.

Thanks to generous government subsidies, Medicare Advantage plans, which cover healthcare as well as prescription drugs, are now more common, more flexible, and less expensive than they had been in the past. Some charge $0 premiums, in addition to the Medicare Part B premium, and can be a good alternative to Medigap.

No longer just Medicare HMOs, some of these plans now let you use any doctor that accepts Medicare (these are called private fee-for-service plans) or large networks of doctors that span several states (regional preferred-provider organizations). To find out about the options in your area, see the Medicare options compare tool at Medicare.gov (*www.medicare.gov/mppf*).

And if your mother has a Medigap policy with prescription drug coverage—plans H, I, or J—then she should definitely consider other options. Those policies provide much less drug coverage—at a much higher price—than the new government-subsidized Medicare prescription drug plans. You can switch to another type of Medigap policy (A through G or the new K and L) and buy a stand-alone Part D drug plan, or switch to a Medicare Advantage plan for all of your medical care. To search for a plan in your area and calculate the costs, go to Medicare.gov's prescription drug plan finder (*www.medicare.gov/mpdpf*).

Even if your mother is happy with her current coverage, it's a good idea to compare prices from other companies. Even though the government created 12 standardized plans (A through L)—with every plan A, for example, offering the exact same coverage—the price range can be huge from company to company. In a 2005 study by Weiss Ratings, the annual premiums for a 65-year-old woman buying plan F ranged from $516 to $10,788 (that's not a typo), even though each policy provided the exact same coverage. Many people pay more than they need to just because they don't know to shop around.

After you pick the letter plan you want, see how the policies are priced. Attained-age policies increase the premiums as the insured ages; issue-age and community-rated policies do not (all three types can raise rates due to health care inflation). It's generally best to buy the lowest-priced issue-age or community-rated policy, which may cost a little more in the beginning (but often does not) but usually doesn't raise rates as high through time. Because the coverage is standardized and the policies merely fill in the gaps left by Medicare, the service rarely varies by company, so you really can shop by price. You can check out prices in your area through the Medicare.gov personal plan finder or through most state insurance departments' Web sites (*www.naic.org*).

Is it worthwhile to sign up for Medicare Part D prescription drug coverage?

U nless you're receiving better prescription drug coverage through a retiree health insurance policy, it's generally a good idea to sign up for Part D drug coverage, even if you don't have many prescription drug costs now.

These plans, first introduced in 2006, are the first in which Medicare has provided any outpatient prescription drug coverage. The plans are offered by private insurers and have several variations and a wide variety of prices. Many companies offer a standard plan that requires you to pay a $265 deductible in 2007, after which the plan covers most prescription-drug bills until the total costs reach $2,400 (including the deductible, if any, your co-payments, and the insurer's share of the cost). Then you are generally on your own until your own out-of-pocket payouts total $3,850 (often called the doughnut hole), after which the plan pays 95 percent of your remaining expenses. Most insurers also offer other plans with extra coverage in addition to a higher premium.

In 2007, the average premium is about $24 per month, and many plans charge less than $20. You can also pay a higher premium in return for more coverage; some plans charge more but cover all or part of the deductible and coverage gap, so you'll have fewer out-of-pocket expenses. Because each company has different premiums, co-pay amounts, and costs for different drugs (usually falling into two or three price tiers), you'll need to run the numbers for your specific medications and dosages and compare total out-of-pocket costs for several companies. To start, use the Medicare prescription drug plan finder tool at Medicare.gov (*www .medicare.gov/mpdpf*).

It's a good idea to sign up for Part D coverage even if you don't have many prescription costs now, so you'll have the insurance in case you end up needing to buy more drugs in the future. Otherwise, you can only sign up for the coverage during each year's open enrollment period—November 15 to December 31—for coverage to take effect on January 1.

If you were already age 65 and didn't sign up by May 15, 2006, you'll also face a penalty if you ever change your mind and want to buy a policy later. In that case, you'll have to pay a penalty of up to 1 percent of the average premium for each month you delayed after that date. (You can avoid that penalty if you have drug coverage that is considered to be at least as good as Medicare's plan, such as most retiree health insurance plans.) You can avoid the penalty by signing up for a barebones policy now, which you can always switch to a more robust policy if you end up needing more medications in the future. Or you could get both your medical and drug coverage through a Medicare Advantage plan, which has some of the lowest premiums but generally has more restrictions.

Run the numbers for your specific medications through the Medicare.gov prescription drug plan finder—both for premiums as well as out-of-pocket costs for current drugs—to pick the best plan for you.

Closing Words

The best thing about this book is that it isn't over when you're finished reading. I continue to write the Ask Kim column in *Kiplinger's Personal Finance Magazine* every month and I answer reader questions twice a week on Kiplinger.com. I'm always looking for timely topics to cover and ways to help more readers, and I look forward to hearing from you. Please check out my column at *www.kiplinger.com/askkim* or write me directly at *askkim@kiplinger.com.*

I'm excited to answer your questions and continue to help you make the most of your money.

Internet Resource Guide

Chapter 1: Retirement Saving

- Kiplinger.com's "tools" section (*www.kiplinger.com/tools*) is filled with calculators to help you figure out whether you're saving enough, which IRA is right for you, the power of boosting your retirement plan contributions, and many other important topics.
- Kiplinger.com's model investment portfolios (*www.kiplinger.com/investing/kport/funds.html*) list our favorite funds for each investing time frame.
- Financial Engines (*www.financialengines.com*) is the best retirement-planning calculator because it uses Monte Carlo simulations, running through thousands of potential investment scenarios and assessing the likelihood that you'll reach your retirement goals. The service generally costs $149.95 per year, but many employers provide access free through their 401(k) advice services.
- The Social Security Administration's Web site (*www.socialsecurity.gov*) includes several benefits calculators to help you estimate how much money you're on track to receive after you retire. The "quick calculator" can give you a general idea, but the "online calculator" will give you a more precise figure. You'll have to input information from your earnings statement, which you

should receive from the Social Security Administration every year around your birthday, but you can also order one at *www.socialsecurity.gov* too.

■ 401khelpcenter.com is one of the best resources for information about 401(k)s. A lot of the articles are targeted toward plan administrators and other professionals, but it's a great way to keep up with new laws and includes excellent tools and "Topics and Collected Wisdom" columns. It also includes the best list of providers for individual 401(k)s for self-employed people.

■ The Employee Benefits Security Administration Web site (*www.dol.gov/ebsa*), from the U.S. Department of Labor, includes rules for protecting retirement plan assets, lists enforcement actions for problem plans, and includes contact information for complaints against plans that aren't making timely contributions or providing access to your money.

Chapter 2: College Planning

■ Savingforcollege.com (*www.savingforcollege.com*) is the best resource for information about 529 plans. It includes details and ratings for every plan and updates on new laws and financial aid strategies.

■ FinAid.org (*www.finaid.org*) is an excellent resource for information about financial aid and scholarships.

■ The Department of Education's financial aid Web site (*http://studentaid.ed.gov*) shows you how to qualify and apply for federal aid and the rules for paying back your loans.

■ The College Board (*www.collegeboard.com*) has great tools to help you find a college, learn about admissions, and track down scholarships.

■ IRS Publication 970, "Tax Benefits for Higher Education" (available at *www.irs.gov*), explains the tax rules for every kind of college-savings plan and tax breaks for college costs.

Chapter 3: Save Money on Insurance

■ The National Association of Insurance Commissioners (*www.naic.org*) includes links to every state's insurance department, which are tremendous resources for information about insurance rules, company complaint records, buying strategies, and often prices. The NAIC's Consumer Information Source (*www.naic.org/cis*) provides statistics on each insurer's complaint records, and its consumer site, Insureuonline.org (*www.insureuonline.org*) has excellent information about insurance needs at every life stage.

■ eHealthInsurance.com (*www.ehealthinsurance.com*) is the best Web site for health insurance quotes. It provides prices quickly and anonymously for several companies.

■ National Association of Health Underwriters (*www.nahu.org*) is the best way to find help when shopping for health insurance. This health insurance agent association can match you up with a broker in your area who works with several companies and can be a particularly good resource if you have any medical conditions.

■ Kiplinger.com's life insurance needs calculator is one of the best resources for figuring out how much life insurance you really need (available at *www.kiplinger.com/tools*).

■ AccuQuote.com and Insure.com are two of the best sources for life insurance quotes. Insure.com even lists the underwriting criteria that insurers use when determining who qualifies for each price. Call AccuQuote at 800-442-9899 for personal service, especially if you have any medical conditions.

- InsWeb (*www.insweb.com*) is one of the best sources for auto insurance quotes. Also check out the Web sites for Progressive (*www.progressive.com*), State Farm (*www.statefarm.com*), and GEICO (*www.geico.com*).

- The Independent Insurance Agents & Brokers of America Web site (*www.iiaba.org*) is the best way to find an independent insurance agent in your area who works with many companies and can help you find the best deals on auto and homeowners' insurance.

- AccuCoverage (*www.accucoverage.com*) provides the best tool for calculating how much homeowners' insurance you need. For $7.95, you get access to the same database of rebuilding costs that insurance companies use. Just input information about your house, its materials, and special features, and you'll see how much coverage you should buy.

Chapter 4: Credit and Debt

- myFICO.com (*www.myfico.com*) is the consumer site for Fair Isaac, the company that developed the credit score most lenders use. It's the best resource for up-to-date figures on how your credit score affects your loan rates, strategies for improving your score, and what your score includes. For a fee, you can also order your score and receive advice about boosting your number.

- AnnualCreditReport.com (*www.annualcreditreport.com*) is the site where you can order one free credit report every 12 months from each of the three credit bureaus. Other sites with similar names generally have hidden fees, such as a requirement that you sign up for a monthly credit monitoring program.

- Equifax (*www.equifax.com*), Experian (*www.experian.com*), and TransUnion (*www.transunion.com*), the three credit bureaus, also include helpful information about your credit record and how to dispute errors.

- CardWeb (*www.cardweb.com*) and Bankrate (*www.bankrate.com*) can help you search for the best credit card deals. The sites also include great calculators that show how long it will take to pay off your balance.

- The National Foundation for Credit Counseling (*www.nfcc.org*) and the Association of Independent Consumer Credit Counseling Agencies (*www.aiccca.org*) can help you find a credit counselor in your area. Also check out the U.S. Trustee's list of approved credit counseling agencies (*www.usdoj.gov/ust*), which have been vetted by the Department of Justice as a result of the new bankruptcy law and can help people even if they aren't about to declare bankruptcy.

- The Federal Trade Commission's Identity Theft site (*www.ftc.gov/idtheft*) is the best resource for reporting identity theft and learning about steps you can take to protect yourself.

Chapter 5: Your Home

- Kiplinger.com's real estate calculators (*www.kiplinger.com/tools*) provide a lot of information to help with your home purchase: you can shop for the best mortgage deals, estimate your monthly payments, calculate how much money you'll save by refinancing, figure out how much house you can afford, and determine how much you can write off each year in interest.

- myFICO.com (*www.myfico.com*), the consumer site for credit-score company Fair Isaac, provides up-to-date figures on how much your credit score can affect your rate.

- The IRS Web site (*www.irs.gov*) has several tax guides explaining the tax breaks for homeownership, including Publication 523, "Selling Your Home," Publication 935, "Home Mortgage Interest Deduction," and Publication 527, "Residential Rental Property."
- The Mortgage Professor's Web site (*www.mtgprofessor.com*) includes excellent information and calculators to help you choose a mortgage, decide whether you should refinance or trade in your adjustable-rate mortgage, and avoid expensive mortgage mistakes.

Chapter 6: Lower Your Taxes

- The IRS Web site (*www.irs.gov*) is the best resource for information about taxes. Use the search feature to find publications explaining the laws covering every tax-related topic.
- Kiplinger.com's tax page (*www.kiplinger.com/money/taxes*) includes timely news about tax-law changes, money-saving advice, state tax profiles, and calculators to help you estimate your taxes and withholding.
- GainsKeeper (*www.gainskeeper.com*) is one of the best ways to keep track of the tax basis on your investments, including splits, spin-offs, and your reinvested dividends.
- ItsDeductible (*www.itsdeductible.com*) helps you value the items you donate to charity and maximize your income-tax deduction.
- The Better Business Bureau's Wise Giving Alliance (*www.give.org*) and Charity Navigator (*www.charitynavigator.org*) are filled with resources to help you check out a charity and review its legitimacy and financial situation.

Chapter 7: Financial Strategies After You've Retired

■ The Social Security Administration Web site (*www .socialsecurity.gov*) has a lot of information about your retirement benefits, including calculators to help you decide when to start taking payouts.

■ T. Rowe Price's Retirement Income Calculator (*www .troweprice.com/ric*) shows how likely you are to run out of money in retirement if you continue to spend at your current pace. The calculator is particularly helpful because it uses Monte Carlo simulations, running through hundreds of investment scenarios and figuring the probability that your savings will last for a particular time period, no matter what happens in the market during that time.

■ Medicare's Web site (*www.medicare.gov*) has excellent calculators to help you find the best Medicare prescription drug plan and Medicare supplement or Medicare Advantage policy, as well as information to help you learn about your coverage and lower your costs. Sign up for MyMedicare.gov to receive personalized information.

■ Medicare Rights Center (*www.medicarerights.org*) also has great advice for making the most of your Medicare coverage and filling in the gaps, with easy-to-read tables explaining what Medicare and each Medigap policy does and doesn't cover.

■ ImmediateAnnuities.com (*www.immediateannuities .com*) is the best source for finding immediate annuities. You type in the amount you want to invest and immediately see the top payouts for annuities that last as long as you or you and a beneficiary live, or for a certain number of years.

Some of the same words keep cropping up again and again in the answers, and it's because they represent some key elements of a good financial plan or important tax breaks that can save you money. Here's what you need to know.

401(k) A 401(k) is one of the most valuable retirement-saving tools. You invest pre-tax money into the account—lowering your taxable income—then taxes are deferred until you withdraw the money in retirement. If you take the money before age 59½, you'll be hit with a 10% early-withdrawal penalty, although you can borrow from your account in certain circumstances.

An added bonus: Most employers match at least part of your contributions, making the 401(k) even more valuable. A typical match is 50 cents for every dollar you contribute up to 6 percent of your salary.

In 2007, you can contribute up to $15,500 in a 401(k), or $20,500 if you're 50 or older.

529 plan A 529 plan is the best way to save for college. The contribution limits are higher than you'd ever need to worry about—generally about $250,000 per beneficiary—there are no income limits to contribute, and you can use the money tax-free for college expenses. You may get a state income-tax deduction for your contributions, which is available in more than half the states. (You generally need to open up a plan in your own state to qualify, although three states now let you take a deduction for contributions to any state's plan.) And you can use the money for any college in the United States and many in foreign countries.

A 529 also gives you a lot of control over the money; you can switch beneficiaries to another relative if the child doesn't go to college or doesn't need the money (or if you just change your mind), and you can get your money back entirely if you decide not to use it for anyone's college, although you will owe taxes plus a 10 percent penalty on your earnings. Most 529s offer a variety of mutual fund choices as well as age-weighted funds, which automatically shift your money to more conservative investments as your child gets closer to college age.

capital gains and losses These are the taxes you pay on your investment profits—which applies to stocks, funds, home-sale profits (above the $250,000 exclusion for singles; $500,000 for couples) and a variety of other investments. If you've owned the investment for more than one year, you'll usually pay long-term capital gains taxes on your profits, which is 15 percent for most people, but five percent for people in the lowest two income-tax brackets. Investments held for less than a year are generally subject to short-term capital gains taxes, which are the same as your income-tax rate. You report capital gains and losses on Schedule D.

cash value life insurance A life insurance policy that provides insurance coverage as well as a savings account. Unlike term insurance, you can keep the policy for the rest of your life, not just 20 or 30 years. There are three main types of cash value insurance: whole life, universal life, and variable universal life. The premiums and fees tend to be a lot higher than they are for term insurance, but they can be helpful for people who need insurance to last for longer than 30 years if, for example, you have a special-needs child who will always be dependent on you, you own a business, or you're worried about estate taxes.

catch-up contributions Extra contributions you can make to your 401(k) and IRA if you're age 50 or older. Instead of a 401(k) limit of $15,500 in 2007, workers age 50 and older can contribute $20,500 to their 401(k)s. At that age, you can also contribute an extra $1,000 to your IRA, giving you a total contribution limit of $5,000 for 2007. Adding the extra money is a great way to catch up on your retirement savings, especially after your kids graduate from college and you finally have more money to save.

COBRA A federal law that requires most companies with 20 or more employees to let you stay on their health insurance plan for a certain time period after you leave the group. You can keep your group health insurance through COBRA for up to 18 months after you leave your job, or can remain on your former spouse's employer plan for up to 36 months after you get divorced. Your children can keep the coverage for up to 36 months after they no longer qualify (generally when they're no longer a full-time student or reach age 25, although the laws recently expanded the eligibility in some states).

COBRA can be a good deal if you have any medical problems because the insurer cannot reject you or raise your rate because of your health. But the price jumps because you have to pay the entire cost yourself, with no subsidy from the employer. If you're healthy, you can generally find a better deal on your own.

Coverdell education savings account Like 529s, Coverdell education savings accounts let you save in a tax-deferred account and use the money tax-free for educational expenses. But unlike 529s, you aren't limited to college costs. You can also use the money for elementary and secondary school tuition, a computer, printer, textbooks, tutoring, educational software, and other expenses, whether your child is in public or private school.

These accounts are a good choice if you want more control over the investments than you'd have with a 529 plan. You can open a Coverdell account at a brokerage firm or mutual fund company, and you generally have the same investment choices as IRAs—often hundreds of funds and stocks. But you can only contribute up to $2,000 per beneficiary per year, and you can only contribute if your adjusted gross income is $110,000 or less if you're single or $220,000 if you're filing jointly. The money must be used by age 30, or you'll owe taxes and a 10-percent penalty on the earnings.

credit score Your credit score, the numerical summary of how much you owe and how promptly you pay your bills, is one of the key factors lenders use when deciding whether to lend you money and determining what rate to charge. A good score can save you thousands of dollars on your mortgage, car loan, and credit card interest payments. A bad score can raise your interest rates, make it tough to get an apartment, and even boost your auto insurance premiums.

FICO scores, the credit scores developed by Fair Isaac that most lenders use, range from 300 to 850. The median score is 723. You'll generally have a different score for each of your credit reports, which is why it's important to check your report at the three major credit bureaus—Experian, Equifax and TransUnion—for errors. The best way to maintain a good score is to pay your bills on time. More than one-third of your score is based on your payment history and another third is based on your "credit utilization," which is the percentage of your credit limit that you've actually used. It's generally best to keep the balance on your cards below 25 percent of your available credit. Go to MyFico.com for more information on how the scores work and what you can do to improve them.

custodial account These accounts, also known as a Uniform Gifts to Minors Act (UGMA) in some states, and a Uniform Transfers to Minors Act (UTMA), are the most common way to open an investment account for a minor. The adult generally controls the money until the child reaches the age of majority (21 in most states, 18 in a few) and can spend it on anything to benefit the minor. In 2007, the first $850 of earnings on the custodial account are tax-free, the next $850 are taxed at no more than 10 percent, and any earnings above $1,700 are taxed at the parents' rate until the child reaches age 18 (before 2006, the child's rate applied starting at age 14).

Custodial assets are considered to be the child's assets in financial aid formulas, and children are expected to contribute 35 percent of their assets for college costs (the number shrinks to 20 percent on July 1, 2007). Parental assets and 529s, on the other hand, are only tapped at 5.6 percent in the financial aid formulas.

deductible The portion of your medical bills that you have to pay out of your own pocket before your insurance kicks in. Raising your deductible on homeowners', health, and auto insurance can cut your premiums significantly, while only raising your out-of-pocket costs if you end up having large claims.

flexible spending account Many employers offer this type of account, which lets employees contribute pre-tax money to pay for uninsured medical expenses or dependent care. The annual contribution limits vary by employer, but are generally $3,000 for medical expenses and $5,000 for dependent care. Employees can then use that money tax-free for child-care costs or medical expenses that aren't covered by insurance, such as health insurance deductibles, co-payments, prescription and non-prescription drugs, eyeglasses, contact lenses, dental work, and in vitro fertilization. You generally must use the money in the account by the end of the year or else lose it, but some employers have extended their deadline until mid-March of the following year.

health savings account You can have a health savings account either through your employer or on your own if you have an individual health insurance policy. To qualify, you must be under age 65 and have an HSA-eligible high-deductible health insurance policy, which requires a deductible of at least $1,100 for individual coverage and $2,200 for families in 2007.

Then, you can open a health savings account and contribute up to a maximum of $2,850 for individual coverage and $5,650 for families in 2007 (people age 55 or older can make an extra catch-up contribution of $800). Your contributions are tax deductible and you can use the money tax-free for medical expenses in any year. Unlike a flexible-spending account, money you don't use in the HSA that year can remain in the account for future expenses. You may have several investing options, including a fixed account and mutual funds. After age 65, you can use the money penalty-free for anything, although you'll have to pay taxes on your earnings for nonmedical expenses.

home-sale exclusion As long as you've lived in your house for two out of the past five years, single people can exclude up to $250,000 in home-sale profits from their taxes, and married couples filing jointly can exclude $500,000. That means a couple who bought a house for $200,000 wouldn't have to pay taxes on the profits unless they sold it for more than $700,000.

If you don't live in the house for two of the past five years, you may still be able to exclude part of your profits from taxes if you had to move for certain reasons (for example, if you take a new job that is more than 50 miles farther away from your home than your old job was or if you move because of death, divorce, or your health). In that case, the exclusion is prorated based on the amount of time you lived in the house. A couple who lived there for only one year, for example, could exclude $250,000 in profits from taxes, which represents half of the $500,000 exclusion because they lived there for half of the two-year requirement.

Hope credit This tax credit can reduce your tax bill by up to $1,650 per child when you pay at least $2,200 in tuition and fees for each child's first two years of college. To qualify, your 2007 adjusted gross income must be less than $94,000 on a joint return (or $47,000 if you're single). The credit amount phases out entirely if you earn more than $114,000 if married filing jointly or $57,000 if filing single. You can't double dip tax benefits, though, so you can only claim the credit if you pay for at least $2,200 of the tuition bill from an account other than a 529 or a Coverdell.

lifetime learning credit After your child's first two years of college, you may qualify for the lifetime learning credit of up to $2,000 per tax return. You have to meet the same income requirements as for the Hope credit, and you have to pay at least $10,000 in college tuition and fees from a source other than a 529 or a Coverdell.

Medicare Part D The government started providing this Medicare prescription drug coverage for the first time in 2006, which is a good idea for Medicare beneficiaries to buy unless they already have better drug coverage through a former employer. The plans are offered by private insurers and have several variations and a wide variety of prices. Many companies offer a standard plan that requires you to pay a $265 deductible in 2007, after which the plan covers most prescription-drug bills until the total costs reach $2,400 (including the deductible, if any, your co-payments, and the insurer's share of the cost). Then you are generally on your own until your own out-of-pocket payouts total $3,850 (often called the doughnut hole), after which the plan pays 95 percent of your remaining expenses. The average plan costs about $24 per month, but most insurers also offer other plans with extra coverage in addition to a higher premium. You can compare premiums and out-of-pocket costs for the Part D plans in your area at *www.medicare.gov/mpdpf.*

Medigap Even though Medicare covers lot of your medical bills after age 65, it still leaves some big gaps, including substantial deductibles, co-payments for doctor visits, and hospital visits. You can buy a separate Medicare supplement policy (also called Medigap) to help fill in those gaps. Medigap plans are sold by private insurers but come in 12 standardized coverage options: plans A through L. Each plan A, for example, provides the exact same coverage, no matter which insurance company sells it. You can generally use any doctor or hospital that accepts Medicare. You'll also need to buy a separate Part D policy for prescription drug coverage.

Another option: Instead of signing up for Medicare plus a Medigap plan and Part D policy, you could get all of your health insurance in one policy through a Medicare Advantage plan. These policies used to be just Medicare HMOs, which limited your coverage to certain doctors and hospitals and weren't a good idea if you traveled frequently or owned a vacation home in another part of the country. But they've recently expanded to include regional preferred provider organizations and even offer some plans—called private fee-for-service—that let you use any doctor anywhere. These policies generally provide coverage for doctors, hospitals, and prescription drugs. The premiums tend to be lower than the cost of Medicare plus a Medigap plan and stand-alone Part D coverage, but you may have more out-of-pocket expenses.

Roth IRA A Roth IRA is one of the best ways to save for retirement. Your contributions to this type of account aren't tax-deductible, but your money grows tax-deferred through the years, and you can withdraw it tax-free in retirement. You can take out your contributions at any time without paying taxes or a penalty and you can withdraw earnings at any age without penalty to pay for college expenses. Additionally, after your account has been open for at least five years, you can withdraw $10,000 in earnings tax and penalty free to buy a first home. Your heirs can inherit a Roth IRA tax free and, unlike traditional IRAs, you don't have to take required distributions at age 70½.

As long as you earn less than $156,000 in 2007 if married filing jointly ($99,000 if single), you can contribute up to $4,000 to a Roth IRA, or $5,000 if 50 or older. You can contribute part of the limit until your income reaches $166,000 (or $114,000 for singles). You can't contribute to a Roth IRA above those income limits.

required minimum distributions After you reach age 70½, you need to start taking withdrawals from your traditional IRAs (these rules don't apply to Roth IRAs). Each year's required minimum amounts are based on your life expectancy. You don't need to take your first IRA distribution until April 1 of the year after the year you turn 70½. But you'll also have to take your distribution for age 71 in that year, too, which you must do by December 31. After that first year, you must make all required minimum distributions by December 31. If you don't withdraw the right amount of money, you'll have to pay a 50 percent penalty on the amount of money you should have withdrawn but didn't.

To calculate how much money you need to withdraw, take the balance of your IRA accounts as of December 31 of the previous year and divide it by the number you'll find in the IRS tables for someone your age. You can use the tables at the end of IRS Publication 590 (available at *www.irs.gov*) or the calculator in the Retirement Tools section of Kiplinger.com.

tax basis Also called "cost basis," this is the amount you paid for an investment. With stocks, for example, it includes the purchase price, brokerage commissions, and any reinvested dividends. You subtract the cost basis from your sale proceeds to determine your taxable gain.

term life insurance This type of life insurance provides coverage for a fixed time period, such as 20 or 30 years. The policy pays out the death benefit if you die during the time period, but generally pays nothing if you're still alive at the end of the term. These policies are popular with families who have young children and only need the insurance until their kids move out or they pay down their mortgage. Many term policies let you lock in the same premium for 20 or 30 years. The premiums are a lot lower than they are for cash value insurance, which includes life insurance and a savings account.

traditional IRA Contributions to this type of IRA may or may not be tax-deductible, depending on your income and if you have another retirement plan at work. Like a Roth IRA, the money grows tax-deferred until retirement. Unlike a Roth IRA, you will have to pay income taxes on your earnings when you withdraw the money after you retire, and will have to start making required minimum distributions after you reach age 70 ½. You'll have to pay a 10% penalty for most withdrawals before age 59½. You can contribute up to $4,000 to a traditional IRA in 2007 (or $5,000 if you're 50 or older), regardless of your income. Those limits apply to either a traditional IRA or a Roth; you can't invest that much in both accounts in one year. If your income is low enough to qualify for a Roth, that's usually a better option than a traditional IRA.

Index